fear not

When life becomes a fugue of fear and a fog of despair and no one gets out of life unfazed and undazed, this book will help you discover how your fears can free you to flee, not from God but to God.

—LEONARD SWEET, best-selling author, professor, and chief contributor to sermons.com

While our circumstances may differ, fear is one of the most common experiences we share in this life. Filled with encouraging testimonies and scriptural references, *Fear Not* carefully and confidently guides us to a place where fear is recognized, understood, and replaced with a courage that can only come from the Lord.

—JO ANNE LYON, General Superintendent, The Wesleyan Church

If you've ever been afraid of what stands in the midst of your journey or overcome with a fear that seems impossible to overcome, this is the guide for you. In *Fear Not*, Ed Love graciously guides us toward an intimacy with God that overcomes the fear and intimidation we so often feel. Along that path he gently nudges us to a place where we find comfort, peace, and the realization that the Lord was with us the entire time.

—CHARLES ARN, professor of outreach and ministry
at Wesley Seminary; author of *Side Door*

Those who fully engage in kingdom living are not necessarily more intelligent or gifted—but they take seriously the biblical invitation to "be strong and courageous." Ed Love guides us into lifting the lid our fears create and courageously experiencing the adventurous life God has for us.

—WAYNE SCHMIDT, vice president, Wesley Seminary at Indiana Wesleyan University

Decisions motivated by fear drive us into the ditch, but we all have our fears. They are often subtle, unnoticeable fears, and we have trouble articulating them. Ed Love uses insightful Scriptures and relevant stories in *Fear Not* to help us begin to receive our Savior's powerful courage and take the wheel back from the fears that drive us.

—DAVID DRURY, chief of staff, The Wesleyan Church; author or coauthor of
several books, including *Being Dad*, *SoulShift*, and *Ageless Faith* (all WPH)

God is asking all of us if we truly trust him. My friend, Ed Love zeroes-in on the issue that courage may well be God's favorite attribute. Success in life often causes individuals to look to themselves for all of the answers. Mr. and Mrs. Fix-It exist on every corner of life. Until life gets tough, that is. As you read this book, consider how God wants to use the storms or delays of today to prepare you for greater things he wants you to accomplish tomorrow.

—JIM DUNN, executive director, Church Multiplication and
Discipleship Division, The Wesleyan Church

Ed Love lives the message of the book because he passionately follows the lead of the one he writes about. "Courage might just be God's favorite virtue" is something that Ed knows by experience through defying the obvious odds for failure and trusting the One who defies the one who is against us—the infernal One who inspires fear. Thanks, Ed for reminding us that we can trust the One who faithfully leads us.

—DENNIS JACKSON, executive director, Global Partners, The Wesleyan Church

If you've ever been afraid, this is the book for you. In *Fear Not*, Ed Love brings to light a subject that most of us struggle with every day. Fear isn't always wrapped up in the big things, it can quietly and quickly leak into our lives, affecting our decisions, attitudes, and interactions. Offering ideas and guidance, Love leads us to a place of confidence that rises above the crippling fear we've experienced and into the life that God intended us to live.

—JEREMY SUMMERS, coauthor of *Awakening Grace*; and director of Spiritual Formation, The Wesleyan Church

There's a big difference between passing along something you learned from someone else and sharing life lessons you've lived from your heart. My friend Ed Love is a good pastor, church planter, thinker, and writer. Each of these chapters start with his own stories of deeply personal life experiences. Then he connects them to the timeless promises of God's Word with great biblical scholarship and sums up each section up with pithy, practical principles that are easy to remember and apply to our own situations. Ed's sharing what he's lived . . . and we all benefit! It's been said that there are 365 "fear not" passages in Scripture . . . start with the ones Ed writes so well about and keep experiencing God's peace every day of your year!

—TIM ROEHL, director of training and development, OMS; author, *TransforMissional Coaching*

Ed's way of writing and explaining stories is straightforward, practical, and packed with thought-provoking nuggets you can use for a lifetime. This book is a must-read!

—TROY A. EVANS, pastor of The EDGE Urban Fellowship; author of *The Edge of Redemption* (WPH)

fear not

Finding Courage to Be Who God Wants You to Be

Ed Love

wphonline.com

Copyright © 2014 by Ed Love
Published by Wesleyan Publishing House
Indianapolis, Indiana 46250
Printed in the United States of America
ISBN: 978-0-89827-912-2
ISBN (e-book): 978-0-89827-913-9

Library of Congress Cataloging-in-Publication Data

Love, Ed (Pastor)
Fear not : finding courage to be who God wants you to be / Ed Love.
    pages cm
Includes bibliographical references.
ISBN 978-0-89827-912-2 (pbk.)
1. Self-actualization (Psychology)--Religious aspects--Christianity. 2. Fear--
Religious aspects--Christianity. I. Title.
    BV4598.2.L68 2014
    242'.5--dc23
                                    2014021161

To my greatest support in life and ministry and the one who
models the way of courage—my wife, Emily Love

contents

Sermon notes and a group leader's guide are available for
download at www.wphresources.com/fearnot.

acknowledgements

I want to thank my wife, my partner, Emily, for having the grace to give me up for the many hours and hours of laboring again and again over the manuscript of the book you now hold in your hand. Her never-ending patience and understanding is an inspiration to me. I also want to thank my children, Jennah, Josiah, and Micah, for teaching me how to live with audacious courage and confidence in God's epic adventure.

My special thanks to Andy Merritt for his hard work, feedback, input, and support through the entire process.

Finally, I offer my thanks to the people who have allowed me to take them on a journey discovering the courage to be all who God has called them to be. In spite of the many mistakes I have often made in leading them into the future, the people I pastor at The Well have proven again and again that we can be confident in God's promises. They have offered me the opportunity to rediscover that God is still in the business of transforming lives from the inside out.

introduction

into the woods

Courage is not simply one of the virtues, but the
form of every virtue at the testing point.

—C. S. Lewis

Fear not, for I am with you; be not dismayed, for I am your God;
I will strengthen you, I will help you, I will uphold
you with my righteous right hand.

—Isaiah 41:10 esv

"Dad, no, no, no! Don't go into the woods! Don't go into the woods!" My son, Josiah, screamed at the top of his lungs. His eyes brimmed with tears of fear. I quickly turned the ATV and headed back into the open meadow. Curious as to why the woods so frightened Josiah, I cut the motor and inquired. "Why don't you want to go into the woods? You know that's where all the fun trails are, right?"

Josiah exclaimed, "Dad, I don't want to get stuck in the water again. I know you'll get stuck! I know you'll get stuck!"

Ah. The root of his fear suddenly became clear to me.

A few months earlier, in the middle of a Michigan winter, Josiah and I had an ATV adventure which ended up marking him deeper than what I could have imagined. Toward the back of our property lie several swampy areas, which are usually frozen solid during the winter months.

On one afternoon thrill ride, I decided to take a risk and drive across the iced-over swamp. Besides a few snaps, crackles, and pops, I arrived on the other side without any problems. The shock came during the second pass.

As I bolted over the frozen water, the ice suddenly began to give way. I tried to maneuver out of it, but the back of the ATV began to sink like the Titanic. As the ice broke beneath us, Josiah tumbled off the back of the vehicle into the subzero water. I quickly leaped into the swamp, grabbed my boy, and with all my might dragged him to safety.

Josiah was pretty shook up in the moment, but once he made it back into the warmth of the house, dried off, and drank some hot chocolate, he calmed down and life went on. He seemingly went back to his normal childhood routines, and I assumed Josiah would

into the woods

forget about his experience in the backwoods. Unbeknownst to me his fears were far from gone; rather they had gone into hibernation. They were hiding just beneath the surface, waiting for another ride into the woods to rouse them from their slumber.

Now, as we attempted to cross the threshold of the woods again, it became apparent that Josiah wasn't ready to risk riding through the swampy territory. For Josiah, reentering the woods was a reminder of something negative and painful in his past.

Josiah's fear was blocking him from future opportunities.

After sensing Josiah's fright and seeing his tears, I didn't want to force him into doing something he didn't want to do. I took him around the field's edge a time or two and then dropped him off at the house.

Later in the evening, as I tucked Josiah into bed, I mentioned his deep fear of the woods. I whispered, "Josiah, you don't have to worry about going back into the woods. There isn't any ice now, and I promise to never get you stuck again. Don't you trust me?"

It took Josiah a few moments to process, but he eventually responded, "Dad, do you promise to never get me stuck in the water again?"

"Of course," I affirmed.

Josiah replied, "OK, Dad, I trust you. We can go into the woods again."

I'm not usually very emotional, but as I heard my son say those three simple words, "I trust you," my heart leaped with joy. With an uncontrollable smile and happy tears slipping down my cheeks, I said, "Josiah, I love how courageous you are. I am so proud of you."

In that quiet father-and-son moment, I began to realize that over-coming our greatest fear isn't really about mustering up the energy to go through the experience again—it's about learning to trust again.

15

danger zone

Life is full of fears, isn't it?

It seems as though at every turn, every stage of life, new fears try to wrap their claws around our hearts and hold us back from fulfilling our greatest potential. Sometimes our inner fears remain in hibernation mode for years. They function like a parasite—continually draining our drive and vision for God's preferred future to unfold in our lives.

There are as many cliché and shallow suggestions for overcoming fears as there are fears themselves. Repeating the mantra, "I think I can, I think I can, I think I can" doesn't get us very far. Neither does "suck it up," "buckle down," and "just persevere." Fear is too strong a foe to be vanquished so easily. There's more to it.

Conquering any internal fear will always involve a sense of trust— ultimately a trust in our heavenly Father and his plan for our lives. God's people have always been called to face their fears, but becoming a fearless follower of God is not easy. Let's be honest, when it comes to facing our fears, our natural tendency is to run and hide.

We are conditioned from a very early age to avoid pain and uneasiness, not run toward it. Yet playing life safe doesn't seem to be God's primary mode of operation. In the biblical narrative, God consistently challenged his servants to step out of comfortable and known circumstances in faith and to enter realms fraught with danger.

In a letter to the church in Corinth, the apostle Paul shared his rather painful life experiences with his church family. Here's a glimpse of Paul's highlight reel:

I've worked much harder, been jailed more often, beaten up more times than I can count, and at death's door time after time. I've been flogged five times with the Jews' thirty-nine lashes, beaten by Roman rods three times, pummeled with rocks once. I've been shipwrecked three times, and immersed in the open sea for a night and a day. In hard traveling year in and year out, I've had to ford rivers, fend off robbers, struggle with friends, struggle with foes. I've been at risk in the city, at risk in the country, endangered by desert sun and sea storm, and betrayed by those I thought were my brothers. I've known drudgery and hard labor, many a long and lonely night without sleep, many a missed meal, blasted by the cold, naked to the weather. And that's not the half of it, when you throw in the daily pressures and anxieties of all the churches. (2 Cor. 11:25–28 MSG)

Does Paul's life and ministry experience sound safe and peaceful? Not so much. Was Paul doing exactly what God created and called him to do? Without a doubt.

Apparently, the most dangerous place to be is right in the center of God's will.

wanting more

When I first believed in God's redemptive work through Jesus, I didn't fully realize what I was being invited into. I thought that if Jesus was saving me, then my life ought to feel easier and run smoother.

I quickly began to feel let down. Not only did it seem like Jesus was not giving me what I wanted, but also that life with Jesus

17

seemed just plain hard. Besides an eternity in heaven, I genuinely wondered if there was any advantage to the Jesus deal.

Consequently, my wondering eventually led to wandering. For several years, I ran from God and dipped into a dark and sinful world. My life without God appeared to be fun and free, but something in my soul was left wanting. My life felt like a black hole, sucking in every possible pleasure and leaving nothing but an empty void in my soul in return.

Just before I left for college, I decided enough was enough. I was ready for a soul shift. After attending a spiritual renewal retreat, I was certain I needed God and God wanted me. I was finally ready to give my life to Christ. And by giving my life to Christ, I didn't just mean in a spiritual sense, but in a physical sense, too. I was ready to go all in.

Like many teens who grow up in a church environment, I had made multiple recommitments to God. However, this time was different. I was finally willing to embrace the fact that life doesn't center on me and my purposes. Rather, everything in my life ought to center on God and his purposes.

Something was clicking in my heart and soul. I couldn't get this new perspective out of my mind. If everything centered on God, then I had to ask myself: What does God want from me? And how might God use me in his purposes? I had never thought to ask those types of questions before. My prayers more typically focused on things I wanted from God, instead of on what God wanted.

As I continued to explore this seemingly radical way of thinking, I had to acknowledge something: If I truly committed to living for God and his purposes, then I must do what God wants me to do, not just what I want to do.

No longer would it be "My will be done"—it would be "Thy will be done."

I knew the biblical storyline well enough to know that God likes to ask his followers to do some pretty crazy things.

God asked Abraham to sacrifice his son Isaac (Gen. 22). God asked Moses to deliver his people from the bondage of the Egyptian pharaoh (Ex. 3). God told Gideon to cut the size of his army from thirty-two thousand to three hundred in order to win a battle (Judg. 7). God asked the Israelites to march around Jericho seven times in order to acquire the city (Josh. 6). God told Hosea to take a prostitute as his wife (Hos. 1). Jesus asked Peter to walk on water (Matt. 14). And God asked his one and only Son, Jesus, to sacrifice his life on a cross in order to absorb the sins of the world. Talk about crazy!

And to think, with every big ask from God, each person was required to overcome some type of inner fear. For Abraham it was the fear of being labeled a child murderer. For Moses it was the fear of living in a foreign land. For Gideon it was the fear of being annihilated. For the Israelites it was the fear of looking like fools. For Hosea it was the fear of being shunned by his contemporaries. For Peter it was the fear of not being capable. And for Jesus it was the fear of death.

These types of crazy faith stories made me curious. Would God ask me to do something crazy? Would God ask me to do something I wasn't naturally good at? Would God ask me to do something I would have chalked up as a life failure? Would I be forced to face my deepest fears?

why not you?

I can recall many dreadful moments throughout my grade-school experience. One that stands out in my memory above the others in terms of stomach-churning prepubescent anxiety was when teams were chosen during recess.

Typically, all the students who wanted to play in a game, like kickball, lined up and then the team captains began sizing up everyone and selecting their players. The strongest and fastest players were always chosen first, and the weaker, slower players, last. The further down the line of choice you were, the larger the hit to your self-esteem. Being picked last felt less like an objective assessment of athletic abilities and more like a soul-crushing life prophesy.

My physical development always seemed to lag behind that of my peers. To make matters worse, I wore size 11 shoes in the fourth grade, so I was always a little uncoordinated and not usually one of the first-round draft picks, if you know what I'm saying.

Not only in sports, but in every area of my life, I seemed to be pretty much average. Eventually I accepted the fact that I was just the average Joe.

When I recommitted my life to Christ, I was shocked to discover that God doesn't function like those kickball team captains. God doesn't size up his children and select the strongest first. In a bizarre way, God often uses the weak links—the underdogs—for his kingdom work.

I can still remember the moments after I sensed the Lord calling me to dedicate my life to building up his church. In the midst of a moonlit stroll down a nature trail, I told God, "I'm ready to serve you. I'll do whatever you ask of me." Instantly, God spoke to the deepest part of my heart and said, "Ed, I want you to build my church."

Rather than a feeling of excitement, my gut reaction was to tell God why he had chosen the wrong guy. "Hold on God," I said. "I know I told you I was willing to do whatever you wanted, but I didn't really mean *whatever*. I'm not a preacher, pastor, or leader. You know me. I'm the shy guy. I'm the introvert. I hate public speaking. I'm not very smart. I'm not good at anything. And I'm certainly not a person of influence. You've got the wrong guy. I'll end up messing up your church. Seriously, God, I'm pretty sure I can't do what you're asking."

I waited a few moments for some sort of response. Maybe I was hoping God would make a case for me. But he didn't. He was silent.

That first response when I sensed God nudging me to dedicate my life to building up his church was to ask, "Who am I, God?" I didn't seem to have any great natural leadership abilities, and I couldn't picture how the Lord might be able to use me in his purposes.

This outlandish ask from God didn't make sense at all, at least not from a human perspective. For weeks, I wrestled with self-doubt and fear. I genuinely wondered if God had his wires crossed. I just did not fit the mold of a church leader. Never in a thousand years could I envision myself leading God's people, and I knew my friends and family would agree!

Nevertheless, I finally submitted to my heavenly Father. In a quiet moment I prayed, "I really don't know how your plans are going to come together, but I will trust you." Immediately, I felt a peace I had never experienced before in my life. I knew I was on the right track. But I also started to wonder how I was going to overcome some of my greatest fears.

run of the mill

One day as I was exploring the Scriptures, I came across an interesting story in Acts 4. Peter and John were preaching and were busted
for inciting civil disruption. Apparently, some leaders within the Jewish religion didn't like discovering that people were finding Peter and
John's message attractive and becoming Jesus followers.

After their arrest, Peter and John were required to go before the
Jewish court of law. In the middle of their trial, Peter rose up, filled
with the Holy Spirit, and shared the salvation message. Peter and
John's courage astonished the leaders. They realized Peter and John
were unschooled, ordinary men, and they also noted that Peter and
John had been with Jesus (Acts 4:13).

This little story grabbed my attention in a big way. God used two
ordinary men to do something extraordinary. Peter and John would
not have been selected in the first-round draft pick. They were just
the average Joes. Then it dawned on me. Two of the most influential
disciples of Jesus were run of the mill! This made me wonder even
more about my life. If Peter and John were considered average and
ordinary, then maybe God could use me after all.

As I saw God's pattern of using those who most people wouldn't
think to use, I wanted nothing more than to demonstrate great courage
like Peter and John. What I didn't realize yet was where there is great
courage, there is also another force at work—a discouraging one.

John 10:10 makes it clear; we have an Enemy who exists to steal,
kill, and destroy our lives. After committing to follow God, it doesn't
take long to realize one of the Evil One's primary tools is to freeze
us with fear. If the Evil One can cause us to lock up, run away, or
continue living mediocre and safe lives, then he has done his job.

If fear is the Evil One's tool, then it makes perfect sense for faith to be God's tool. Second Timothy 1:7 says, "For God did not give us a spirit of fear, but of power, and of love, and of a sound mind" (YLT).

God has given his faithful followers access to catalytic courage!

God's favorite virtue

Courage is admirable, isn't it? We love to tell stories of people who embraced their fears and stepped into the realm of courage.

Do you remember the story of Chesley Sullenberger? The plane he was flying was disabled shortly after takeoff when it struck a flock of Canada geese. He then successfully executed an emergency landing in the Hudson River, saving all 155 passengers and crew who were onboard that day. It was amazing.

Or, do you remember the story of the Chilean miners who were trapped underground for sixty-nine days? It was incredible. All of the miners were rescued.

Or, do you remember the story of Aaron Ralston? He survived a canyoneering accident where a boulder fell onto his hand. After 127 hours, Aaron finally dislodged himself by amputating his own forearm with a dull multi-tool. Unbelievable!

You see, we love to capture and share stories of courage. And so does God.

God's courage is more than human ingenuity or initiative. God's courage gives us the ability to conquer fear and, in a strange twist of irony, allows us to fulfill our greatest potential in life.

Courage just might be God's favorite virtue. God loves to see his people abandon their self-interests, rise up in courage, and trust

(23)

in his plan. Wouldn't it be remarkable if the world equated being Christian with being courageous?

I'll be the first to admit, I struggle with the pursuit of courage. In my human nature, I prefer to be comfortable. I don't enjoy taking risks which invoke emotional, psychological, or physical pain. I would rather take life easy and do the bare minimum. I would rather not lead my family in the ways of Jesus. I would rather not be in front of people communicating God's redemptive story. I would rather not plant new churches. I would rather not start a new ministry. I would rather not continue to build up Christ's church.

Why? Because I am forced to face my greatest fears!

Even though courage isn't my default disposition, I am always amazed by the inner fulfillment which comes from conquering my fears. This sense of fulfillment is worth every moment of tension and turmoil.

a summoning

Are you beginning to see the connection between your spiritual growth and conquering those fears that hold you back from fulfilling your greatest potential?

Maybe the Evil One has frozen you with fear. Maybe you have pictures of the past when you took great risks for God, but have no dreams of the future. Maybe you are stuck in your spiritual growth. Maybe you feel like there must be more to this Christian life. Maybe you need to learn how to trust again. If you have any of those feelings, then you have the right book in your hands.

Perhaps it's time to look within and ask yourself, "What inner fears are holding me back from fulfilling my greatest potential?"

Throughout this book, we will explore many of the New Testament stories where God or his messengers commanded an individual to "Fear not!" Each chapter will expose a different fear common to humanity. At the end of the journey, you will have a clearer understanding as to how you can overcome your deepest fears and allow God to accomplish his great purposes through your life.

As we journey together, I'll be honest with you about my fears, and I hope you'll be honest with yourself as well. Perhaps, with God's help, we can learn how to conquer our fears, trust God more, and fulfill our greatest potential.

1

when God's ideas seem impossible

Expect great things from God;
attempt great things for God.

—WILLIAM CAREY

The Lord is my light and my salvation—
whom shall I fear? The Lord is the stronghold
of my life—of whom shall I be afraid?

—PSALM 27:1

One moment I'll never forget was when a local youth pastor called me and asked me to speak to his youth group. I had shared with a few of my friends how I was preparing to go to a Bible college and study youth ministry, but I was certainly not a recognized youth speaker in the area. At the time, I honestly didn't know why this particular youth pastor felt compelled to ask me to speak to his teens.

Never in a million years would I have pictured myself sharing my life story and teaching God's Word in front of people. I was the shy kid who tucked behind my parents when people tried to make small talk with me. I hated public speaking with a passion. Nothing frightened me more than having a group of people looking at me. I even dreaded the moment when teachers would take attendance and I was required to say, "Here," after they announced my name. Simply put, I was not a communicator, and I had no desire to be one.

When the youth pastor asked if I would speak to his students, everything inside me screamed, "No way!" So imagine my surprise when I heard the word "Sure" slip out of my mouth.

I had no sooner hung up the phone than I once again began giving God a litany of reasons why this was a mistake. "This is a terrible idea, God. What if I freeze up? What if I forget the punch line? What if my zipper is down? What if some kid falls asleep?" From every angle I looked at it, speaking to people did not seem like a good idea. I was sure to fail. Yet I couldn't shake the feeling that God wanted me to do it. Some comfort came from the fact that if I failed, at least I could say, "It wasn't my idea!"

I had two weeks before my newfound date with destiny, and during that time fear not only nipped at my heels, but tried to consume my being. It seemed impossible to overcome. Those two weeks of prayer and preparation dragged by with agonizing slowness. Thoughts of being in front of people caused me intense anxiety, not to mention sleepless nights. After writing and rewriting my message more times than I could count, I finally gave it to God and in jest said, "God, you know I need a miracle on this one!"

it's possible

Even though this unexpected foray into the world of speaking caused my stomach to somersault and my body to toss and turn all night, something was compelling and propelling me to stay the course. I knew I was breaking through a deep fear of mine and maybe, just maybe, God was going to use it for his good purposes.

Something impossible was being made possible.

In the book of Luke, we read about a man named Zechariah. Zechariah was the father of John the Baptist, the wild man who prepared the way for the Lord Jesus. By the time Zechariah and his wife, Elizabeth, came onto the scene, many God-followers were beginning to lose hope in God's future plans for his people. It seemed like the sell-by date on God's promises had expired, and that all the people were left with was rotten milk.

The story of Zechariah is a story about God making the impossible possible. What God did in Zechariah's and Elizabeth's lives was a significant foreshadowing of what God would soon do in and through Jesus' earthly parents, Joseph and Mary. In Zechariah's life, God made a small move with little John before he made his big move with Jesus. In a unique way, God was preparing his people and building up their confidence that he was at work.

Here's the story of Zechariah and a glimpse into his preparation phase:

Then an angel of the Lord appeared to [Zechariah], standing at the right side of the altar of incense. When Zechariah saw him, he was startled and was gripped with fear.

But the angel said to him: "[Fear not], Zechariah; your prayer has been heard. Your wife Elizabeth will bear you a son, and you are to call him John. He will be a joy and delight to you, and many will rejoice because of his birth, for he will be great in the sight of the Lord. He is never to take wine or other fermented drink, and he will be filled with the Holy Spirit even before he is born. He will bring back many of the people of Israel to the Lord their God. And he will go on before the Lord, in the spirit and power of Elijah, to turn the hearts of the parents to their children and the disobedient to the wisdom of the righteous—to make ready a people prepared for the Lord."

Zechariah asked the angel, "How can I be sure of this? I am an old man and my wife is well along in years."

The angel said to him, "I am Gabriel. I stand in the presence of God, and I have been sent to speak to you and to tell you this good news. And now you will be silent and not able to speak until the day this happens, because you did not believe my words, which will come true at their appointed time."

Meanwhile, the people were waiting for Zechariah and wondering why he stayed so long in the temple. When he came out, he could not speak to them. They realized he had seen a vision in the temple, for he kept making signs to them but remained unable to speak. (Luke 1:11–22)

Let me give you a bit of context for this story. Zechariah was a Jewish priest. He belonged to the priestly section of Abia. Every direct descendent of Aaron was automatically a priest. This meant that for all ordinary priestly functions there were far too many priests. They were therefore divided into twenty-four sections.

In addition to the three major Jewish celebrations, each priest was only on duty for two weeks out of the year. Most priests looked forward to their two weeks of service. It was likely the highlight of their lives.

During Zechariah's era, there were approximately twenty thousand priests altogether, which meant there were almost one thousand priests per section. Each of the temple duties would be distributed among these thousand priests by a lottery system.

One of the most valued duties of a priest was the privilege of offering the morning or evening incense to God. It was quite possible many priests would never have the honor of burning the incense during their lifetime. However, on this particular day, Zechariah won the lottery! This was the day Zechariah had been dreaming of, and he must have been thrilled to the core of his being. Within this moment, the impossible was becoming possible.

Nonetheless, Zechariah and Elizabeth had one big problem in their lives. They were childless. Infertility in the first-century era was tragic. Believe it or not, childlessness was grounds for divorce.

Some Jewish rabbis said there were seven people who were excommunicated from God. The list began with, "A Jew who has no wife, or a Jew who has a wife and who has no child." You see, childlessness led to hopelessness.[1]

We can imagine that, for many years, one of Zechariah and Elizabeth's daily cries to God was, "Please allow us to have a child. Please allow us to have a child!"

Since Zechariah was a priest, his problem was amplified. Anxiety-producing thoughts most likely plagued him. He probably wondered things like: Am I not being faithful to God? Am I not a good priest? Or, is God mad at me?

By the time Zechariah had the privilege of offering the incense in the temple, he was well along in years. He had most likely given up on the idea of his family tree continuing through his genes.

Nevertheless, as Zechariah entered the temple and faced the altar of incense, God's messenger came to him and said those two life-changing words—*fear not*. The messenger then told him, "Your prayer has been heard. Your wife Elizabeth will bear you a son." After this, the text says, Zechariah was gripped with fear.

Imagine what was going through Zechariah's mind. Not only was a messenger from God in his presence, but a lifelong prayer was being answered in a miraculous way.

What is more, this baby of his was described as no ordinary baby. His baby would be connected to God's redemptive plan for the world. A personal prayer was being answered, but this was more than just personal—a collective prayer was also being answered for all of God's people. This baby was a huge bundle of joy.

I suppose Zechariah's response, "How can I be sure of this?" was only normal. I mean, Zechariah's wife was probably the age of most grandmas and he was being told she was going to have a baby. I know I'd be thinking somebody in the room had been inhaling too much incense!

Even so, Zechariah wanted some evidence of God's seriousness. In Zechariah's mind, what the messenger said was impossible. So he questioned God, which, we discover, is a big no-no. Zechariah obtained his proof, but not in an ultrasound photo. The messenger proved it by muting his vocal chords until the day his son was named.

Making Zechariah speechless may seem like an odd way to discipline him for not immediately embracing God's crazy plan. However, a deeper message was unfolding in the story. God doesn't mind receiving questions, but he doesn't like to be questioned.

Questioning God is a sign of distrust.

Since God desires a relationship with his people and trust is the foundation of any good relationship, we can see how God's reprimand is justified. It's quite possible God wanted Zechariah to remain silent and spend time reflecting on his trust issues, as he learned to embrace the impossible.

believing versus trusting

Recently, I was swimming in a hotel pool with my children. My two older children were leaping off of the edge and dropping into the pool cannonball-style. My youngest son, Micah, is a bit more timid. He was extremely nervous about jumping into the pool on his own. He would approach the edge, but then run backward terrified.

I could tell Micah really wanted to be like his older siblings. However, something was holding him back. I moved closer to the edge and yelled, "Hey Micah, jump to me. I'll catch you!"

After several warm-up attempts, Micah finally leaped into my arms.

"See Micah, it's not hard; you can do it," I asserted.

A giant smile displayed on his face as he said, "I did it, Daddy. I did it!"

33

Then I lifted him up over the edge, and before I even had time to get ready to catch him, he jumped cannonball style into the pool without a second thought. I scooped him up just before the water swallowed him, and he said, "Do it again, again, Daddy!"

After about the twentieth time I lifted him up over the edge, it dawned on me—it wasn't Micah's belief of being able to jump into the water that allowed him to overcome his fear; it was his ability to trust his father's arms of love.

Part of our confusion about how to overcome an inner fear stems from a failure to recognize the difference between belief and trust. Believing in something is different from trusting someone. We may believe something to be true, and it may be. Yet if we don't act on that belief, it doesn't make much difference. Trust, on the other hand, lets us act. It's a proven confidence in someone that allows fear to be set aside. Belief alone doesn't do that. So what makes overcoming an inner fear possible is when we learn to trust our heavenly Father's arms of love.

Often we believe certain things about God, but we don't fully trust him. We might believe God is good, but we don't trust him to do something good. We might believe God is for us, but we don't trust he will be with us. We might believe God is more powerful than the Evil One, but we don't trust in his ability to fight our battle for us in the spiritual realm.

George MacDonald is noted as having said, "To be trusted is a greater compliment than being loved." God doesn't just want our adoration or belief—God wants our trust.

But developing trust takes a lot of time.

time to listen

From relational experience, we know trust does not develop overnight. Deep relational trust might take years to obtain, and it always takes listening ears.

Genuine listening has become a lost art in our culture. Even on a day during which we are in constant contact with people, we rarely take the time to truly hear people out and understand where they are coming from. Have you ever noticed how quickly people cut in on conversations or try to finish another person's sentences?

It makes sense that one reason God silenced Zechariah for nine long months was because God wanted him to spend some time working on their sacred trust. It is quite possible Zechariah had fallen into a bad habit of cutting God off. God knew Zechariah would need an extended period of time to retune his hearing aids.

I'm afraid, much like Zechariah, we too tend to cut off God and don't take the time we should to hear him out.

Think about your God-experiences throughout your lifetime for a moment. When were the times you felt like God was speaking to you or calling you into deeper levels of transformation? I suspect they were times when you shut your yapper and were in listening mode. In most of my spiritual growth experiences, God just so happened to break through to me during times when I was removed from my regular pace of life and had space to be silent.

Silence has a way of leading us to salvation.

Zechariah needed to learn a few things about how God works in order for him to overcome his fears. He needed to learn how to trust in God and God's timing.

When we live in a rush-rush world, it's hard to remain hush-hush. However, remaining in a listening posture for an extended period of time is precisely what allows us to release our fears and see our situation from God's perspective.

side-mirror living

Inscribed on most side mirrors on vehicles there is a small note which reads, "Objects in mirror are closer than they appear." The reason side-mirror makers decided to insert this warning is because the mirror was intentionally made to collect a large field of view, causing objects to look small or more distant. Since the mirror collects a larger scope of images, the actual objects are closer than they seem.

As we attempt to deal with our fears, it's good to keep this in mind; God's perspective is kind of like what we see in our side mirrors. When we listen and look into the side mirror of our life, we will discover God's view on our lives has a much wider scope than ours. In a unique way, God's perspective shows us things we are likely to overlook from our vantage point.

Recently, I was invited to participate in a chapel service at a prison in our area. The service was for level four inmates, which is the level reserved for those who did something really bad.

Many times, I have read Hebrews 13:3 which says, "Continue to remember those in prison as if you were together with them in prison, and those who are mistreated as if you yourselves were suffering." Yet, in the past, something always blocked me from actively engaging with prisoners. Ministering in the prisons didn't seem to fit my purposes. Not to mention I just didn't feel comfortable in the prison setting.

Finally, after two years of processing, I decided to face my fears and go for it. On the day of the event, I was as nervous as a cat in a dog house. I was hoping a good excuse would rise up, but nothing presented itself. I was going to prison whether I liked it or not. As I approached the gates, I said a prayer and asked God to be with me. There was no turning back.

The prison guards patted me down and whisked me away to the chapel area. In a unique way, when I entered the chapel room, my fears vanished. I knew I was in the right place at the right time.

The service was powerful, and the inmates were drawn closer to God. At the end of the gathering, several men boisterously came up to me and thanked me for being there and for blessing them with my words.

As I departed the prison, I then saw God's side-view mirror. I wondered how many times in my life inner fear and my selfish disposition held me back from being a blessing to others.

Like Zechariah, we constantly face fears associated with things we perceive as impossible. Imagine what life could look like if we truly believed nothing is impossible with God (Luke 1:37).

ideas to remember

God likes to make the impossible, possible.
Everything good requires preparation.
To be trusted is a greater compliment than being loved.
More time with God will lead to deeper levels of trust.
God will use us to bless others as we overcome our fears.

questions to discuss

What inner fear seems impossible to overcome?

Why do you struggle to trust God with the outcome in that area?

How much space and time do you carve out of your life in order to listen to God's promptings?

When it doesn't feel good to overcome the impossible, how will you push through the anxiety and tension?

To whom might you be a blessing by overcoming your fears?

2

when you
feel
inadequate

Since fear is unreasonable, never try to reason
with it. So-called "positive thinking" is no weapon
against fear. Only positive faith can rout the
black menace of fear and give life radiance.

—MARION HILLIARD

Do not tremble; do not be afraid. Did I not proclaim my
purposes for you long ago? You are my witnesses—is there
any other God? No! There is no other Rock—not one!

—ISAIAH 44:8 NLT

Have you ever felt utterly inadequate?

Maybe you were overlooked at work and someone else got the promotion. Or maybe you're a stay-at-home mom and wonder if your kids are growing in the right direction. Or maybe you lost your job and wonder if you're good at anything else.

We've all questioned whether or not we bring any value to the world. We've all wondered if we have what it takes. We've all felt moments of inadequacy.

My very first ministry assignment was to oversee the eighth-grade boys' Sunday school class in our church. As you can imagine, there weren't many people signing up for the job, so there wasn't much of an interview process. The pastor of my church basically said, "Ed, we need you to oversee our eighth-grade boys' Sunday school class. Sound good?" Luckily for him, I was in a spot where I was ready for a faith challenge and the idea of leading ten to fifteen boys sounded kind of fun. Little did I know what I was getting myself into!

As I entered the classroom on the first day, I realized I had no clue how to manage a mob of eighth graders. Even more, I had no idea how to teach them anything valuable. I was quickly confronted with my inadequacies. From the moment I accepted the responsibility, I felt like I didn't have what it would take to lead those boys. After all, I was only nineteen years old and still growing in my walk with God.

After our first class, which didn't go the way I had planned, I genuinely wondered if I was the wrong man for the job. I remember praying on the way home, "God, there is no way I can do this task. I'm not good enough. I'm not worthy enough. I'm not old enough. I'm not skilled enough. And I don't have a clue what I'm doing!"

Then in the middle of my woe-is-me moment, I heard the Lord say, "Ed, that's why I chose you."

A smile appeared on my face.

I was beginning to discover what the apostle Paul meant when he said, "Therefore I will boast all the more gladly about my weaknesses, so that Christ's power may rest on me. That is why, for Christ's sake, I delight in weaknesses, in insults, in hardships, in persecutions, in difficulties. For when I am weak, then I am strong" (2 Cor. 12:9–11).

When it came to leading those eighth-grade boys, I was fearful on many levels. I was fearful of not being received well. I was fearful of someone finding out I didn't have everything together in my life. I was fearful of teaching the Bible when I was just beginning to discover God's truth myself. I had numerous fears and many reasons to feel inadequate.

Nevertheless, I was learning how to delight in my weaknesses.

who, me?

Just after the story of Zechariah, there is another account in Luke's gospel which demonstrates how God can use those who feel utterly inadequate.

In Luke 1:26–40, we read about Mary as she received her miraculous pregnancy notification. Here is Mary's marvelous experience:

In the sixth month of Elizabeth's pregnancy, God sent the angel Gabriel to Nazareth, a town in Galilee, to a virgin pledged to be married to a man named Joseph, a descendant of David. The virgin's name was Mary. The angel went to her and said, "Greetings, you who are highly favored! The Lord is with you."

Mary was greatly troubled at his words and wondered what kind of greeting this might be. But the angel said to her, "[Fear not], Mary; you have found favor with God. You will conceive and give birth to a son, and you are to call him Jesus. He will be great and will be called the Son of the Most High. The Lord God will give him the throne of his father David, and he will reign over Jacob's descendants forever; his kingdom will never end."

"How will this be," Mary asked the angel, "since I am a virgin?"

The angel answered, "The Holy Spirit will come on you, and the power of the Most High will overshadow you. So the holy one to be born will be called the Son of God. Even Elizabeth your relative is going to have a child in her old age, and she who was said to be unable to conceive is in her sixth month. For no word from God will ever fail."

"I am the Lord's servant," Mary answered. "May your word to me be fulfilled." Then the angel left her.

At that time Mary got ready and hurried to a town in the hill country of Judea, where she entered Zechariah's home and greeted Elizabeth.

If there was anybody who had a human reason to feel inadequate, it would have been Mary. Here God's messenger revealed to her how God wanted to usher in his plan of salvation for all humanity through her body. Keep in mind, Mary was young, most likely between the ages of twelve and fifteen.

The messenger caught Mary off guard. During Mary's panic attack, the messenger declared those two life-changing words— *fear not*.

Mary had plenty of reasons to be fearful. She was a typical teenage girl, hoping to land a solid man who would build her a strong family. Most women in the first century did not have any aspiration in life other than to be a good mother. Being a mother was synonymous with being blessed.

Never in Mary's wildest dreams would she have thought she would play such a vital role in God's story. It wasn't like Mary grew up in a royal household, knowing she would eventually give birth to the next king. No. Mary would have every reason to think, "Who, me?"

In this holy moment, we can imagine Mary felt extremely inadequate, but regardless of how she felt, she confidently responded, "I am the Lord's servant."

Mary's response tips us off to the fact that she was living in a posture of readiness. She was ready to be used by God. She didn't know it, but she had been preparing for that day for many years.

on your mark, get set, go!

Every four years, the very best athletes from all over the world come together to compete and show the world their talent in the Olympic Games. The world watches in sheer amazement as records are broken and medals are tallied.

Whenever I watch the Olympics, I ponder what it would be like to be in their position. It's a bit of a fantasy, I suppose, but I've always

43

wondered what it would feel like to stand on the winner's podium while my national anthem is being played.

Many of these impeccable athletes train their entire lives for that one Olympic competition. They constantly live in training mode, and when the big day arrives, they are ready to go.

In the same way, God desires for us to live in training mode, so when he calls we are ready to go.

Mary was kind of like an Olympic athlete. However, Mary wasn't committed to a competition—she was committed to walking with God and remaining faithful. For years, Mary was caught up in God's story and immersed in his ways. The story captured in Luke is just our moment to watch Mary go to the winner's circle and receive her reward for her faithfulness.

Don't you love hearing stories of people who worked diligently for years, and then finally reached a moment when they broke through? It's as if they had spent years tunneling through the earth, not knowing if or when they would break through, then suddenly, a stream of light pours in with their last shovelful. Very rarely do we come across a story of pure luck. Most of the time, the people who experience breakthroughs are those who had plenty of moments of feeling broken, abandoned, and confused.

Mary's story reminds us that we ought to spend less time worrying about whether we feel successful and more time preparing.

unfailing words

There are times when I doubt God. I am very aware of God's promises, but sometimes God's vision seems incredibly unrealistic.

In 2005 God called me to plant a new church. I was twenty-five years old and certainly did not feel equipped for the task. I'll be honest—I wasn't! I felt entirely inadequate. I constantly struggled with how others might perceive me, and I wondered if anyone in their right mind would follow me.

As the years went by, the Lord proved himself faithful. Much to my surprise, our new church became firmly planted in God's kingdom soil.

Life and ministry was good, but I noticed I was beginning to lose my passion for reaching the missing. In order to regain my passion for those who were far from God, I began studying every place in Scripture where Jesus went out of his way to pursue people. This is a very dangerous study, by the way. Once again, God began to break my heart for the lost.

As a result of my study, I ended up teaching a four-week series on Jesus' parable of the lost sheep and began challenging our church to go into their circles of influence and reach those who were far from God. One Sunday while I was teaching, God spoke to my heart and I sensed a call to reach another community with the message of Jesus.

Believe it or not, the Spirit even revealed the precise community I was to go into. My heart was torn. Nothing in me wanted to plant another church. Planting a new church is hard work!

For fear of being beat up by my church, I didn't share this revelation for quite a while. I let God's call linger as I wrestled with its implications. I'm not one to rush into anything, but I couldn't shake God's prompting. I knew God wanted another new work to rise up, and I knew this was my next assignment.

It wasn't easy when my wife and I finally shared the call God had placed on our lives, but the church gave us their blessing. As we launched out on our new adventure, with three kids in tow, we were terrified. Nothing about this new project looked easy. We would be entering a broken community. It was marred by three broken church plants. There were limited finances. And there was no facility in sight.

We eventually scrounged up a rugged band of twelve who were willing to step out in faith with us. With nothing but faith in our pockets, we began meeting and praying for God to do a good work.

During our early phases, we met in several odd buildings. One was a Styrofoam recycling warehouse. Another one was an old house. The most unique was a daycare facility. However, every location seemed like a far stretch as a place to connect with the community. At one point, I remember wishing I were an ostrich. If I could just bury my head in the ground, then all of my problems would disappear. Everything about this project seemed difficult.

To make matters worse, when I recalled my former office and modern facility, resentment burned in my heart. I wondered why in the world God would call me to something only to fail. Feelings of inadequacy flooded my mind and heart, much like the moments after my first Sunday school lesson with the eighth-grade boys.

And then I remembered.

God had proven himself faithful in my first speaking engagement. God had proven himself faithful in my first Sunday school session. God had proven himself faithful in my first church plant. Time and time again, God had proven himself faithful. Would God not prove himself faithful again?

I knew I needed to pour out my heart to God, so I set aside a large chunk of time and laid out everything before him. I shared every feeling of inadequacy I had felt going into this new adventure, and I asked God to fill me. I don't know how God accomplished it, but in my prayer-filled moment, every feeling of inadequacy vanished. God affirmed the vision in my heart, and I knew he was going to do a good work. All God wanted from me was to be faithful.

count on it

We spend enormous amounts of time on social media tweeting, friending, liking, and poking. We can generate friends in a flash. Yet, sadly, if true friendship is defined as someone we can count on, then we probably don't have very many friends. People we can count on are rare. But when it comes to God, he can always be counted on. When God says he's going to do something, then he's going to do it. We might struggle with God's timeline, but when God says, "Count on it," then we can most certainly count on it.

In Mary's story, after God's messenger shared the pregnancy news, the messenger summed up the message by saying, "and no word from God will fail." It might sound ridiculous to have a baby without . . . you know—but no word from God will fail. God's word can be trusted.

We live in a day where we don't put much stock in people's words. In days past, people would give their word and shake hands to create a legal agreement. But those days are long gone. Nowadays, we must require everything to be in writing so it can be upheld in a court of law. We struggle to trust anybody, even those with whom we are close.

Over time, living in a culture of distrust inevitably affects the way we interact in our relationships. After we've been burned a time or two, we become quick to raise our walls and lower our trust at the slightest hint of trouble. We do this all the time with people, but we also unknowingly do this to God.

For many of us, coming back to God isn't really about reaccepting God's grace—it's about accepting the fact that God can be counted on.

In Mary's response to the messenger, we see a very different perspective than Zechariah's. Remember, Zechariah questioned God, but Mary promptly responded with, "I am the Lord's servant. May your word to me be fulfilled." What an incredible statement!

All too often, our feelings of inadequacy are controlled by our inner fears. Mary shows us how to break through our fear to wholeheartedly trust God instead of wallowing in our inadequacy. Mary heard God's radical calling on her life and responded, "May your word to me be fulfilled."

What would happen in our lives if we allowed Mary's type of faith to unfold?

accepting our call

Once we embrace God's unfailing words, we must learn to accept God's call and follow through, fully believing in his plans.

When I think back on my calling to leave my comfort zone and plant another church, I see another dynamic at work and another individual who was experiencing God's call too.

I'll never forget the moment when the Spirit of God made it clear how my right-hand man, Duane, would continue to advance the mission of our first church plant.

One Sunday, Duane was preaching, and I was back in the tech booth soaking up the moment. As Duane was sharing, the Spirit whispered to me and said, "Duane is going to be the leader of this church." Tears started streaming down my face, because I knew what this meant. It was time to pass the torch.

As you can imagine, my heart was panged and pining all at the same time. But I knew God was up to something good.

In the days after Duane's message, he couldn't shake the feeling of being called to devote his life to building up Christ's church, even if it required great sacrifice. This midlife shift wasn't easy for Duane, since he had a family of five and a good-paying job. Yet he was willing to be like Mary.

Even though Duane was an unschooled and ordinary guy, people were taking note that he had been with Jesus. After a time of discernment, the church affirmed his call to take the leadership reins and confirmed my call to be sent out.

If we were being honest, both of us were wrestling with our fears and felt entirely inadequate for the journey ahead. For me, it was the fear of entering into unknown territory and facing possible failure. For Duane, it was the fear of not knowing what he was doing and facing the possibility of taking his family of five into financial ruin. Neither of us felt worthy to advance in our calling, but we couldn't deny God's call and impeccable timing.

It's not easy overcoming our feelings of inadequacy, but when we do, it's amazing to watch how the Lord comes through.

ideas to remember

God enjoys using our weaknesses.

Be worthy and willing.

Faithfulness will lead to fruitfulness.

We can count on God to fulfill his word.

God calls those who don't feel adequate.

questions to discuss

When was a time when you felt inadequate to do something for God?

When have you seen God use someone's weaknesses to accomplish his purposes?

Have you ever run from God's unique call on your life? What was the result?

Do you struggle to trust God's words? Why?

What inadequacies do you need to confess?

What call from God do you need to embrace?

3

when bad news
is about
to hit home

Faith attracts the positive.
Fear attracts the negative.

—Ed Cole

They do not fear bad news; they confidently
trust the Lord to care for them.

—Psalm 112:7 nlt

There was once a day when I enjoyed getting my mail.

When I first established my own residence, I loved pulling up to my mailbox and opening mail that had my name on it, even if it was junk mail. However, it didn't take long to realize, most of my mail was of a different sort—bills. What was once something I enjoyed quickly turned into a daily moment of anxiety. Nowadays, I have this dreadful fear creep over me as I approach the mailbox, because I know somebody is going to want their money.

Sometimes life seems like the mailbox, doesn't it? A steady stream of expectations, deadlines, and burdens wait for us just around the corner. We never know when they will be "delivered." Often it can seem as though for every step forward you take two steps back. Have you wondered if you'll ever get ahead or if the stream of bad news will ever stop?

As a pastor, I am constantly made aware of everyone's painful situations. Apparently, one of my roles in the body of Christ is to be a sponge and absorb people's bad news. From time to time, when I'm in a worship gathering, I'll break down simply because of the overwhelming weight on me from knowing about everyone's dire state of affairs.

Recently, I was in a discussion forum and someone was sharing about a friend who is afraid to talk to people. She noted her friend had only two acquaintances in life. When she asked her friend why he had isolated himself, he said, "I fear people talking to me, because they may bring bad news into my life." That's interesting, isn't it? The fear of bad news had caused this individual to push away people and limited his potential in life.

This situation may sound extreme, but there are times we, too, live in fear of bad news. If we're not careful, this fear will force us into isolation and limit our influence in the world.

opposite day

In Luke 2:8–12, we read about some shepherds who were being challenged to overcome their fear of receiving bad news. For once, they were on the receiving end of some good news—real good news. Here is their story:

And there were shepherds living out in the fields nearby, keeping watch over their flocks at night. An angel of the Lord appeared to them, and the glory of the Lord shone around them, and they were terrified. But the angel said to them, "[Fear not]. I bring you good news that will cause great joy for all the people. Today in the town of David a Savior has been born to you; he is the Messiah, the Lord. This will be a sign to you: You will find a baby wrapped in cloths and lying in a manger."

It's a wonderful thing to know that the first birth announcement came to a bunch of rugged shepherds.

Shepherds were despised by most of first-century society, especially among the Jewish people. Since shepherds worked closely with sheep and could rarely leave their flocks, they were unable to observe the meticulous hand washing and regulatory details of Jewish ceremonial law. For this reason, most Orthodox Jews despised the shepherds and considered them second-class citizens.

In this story, these particular shepherds may have been quite unique. Every morning and evening, in the Jewish temple, an unblemished lamb was offered as a sacrifice to God. To make sure a supply of perfect lambs was always available, the temple overseers managed

53

their own private flocks of sheep.[1] Paradoxically, the temple overseers would employ the exact people they despised to watch over their special sheep. Go figure.

We know the temple flocks were pastured near Bethlehem, where Mary gave birth to Jesus. It is highly likely these shepherds were responsible for the flocks from which the temple offerings were selected.

Isn't it interesting that the shepherds, who may have looked after the sacrificial lambs, also had the privilege of being the first ones to hear about the sacrificial Lamb of God who takes away the sins of the world?

For shepherds, good news was a rarity. If anyone took time to visit them out in the fields, it was probably to deliver bad news. Notice God's messenger greeted the shepherds with those two life-changing words—*fear not*. There was no need to fear bad news, for the messenger was filled with good news. No wonder the shepherds ran into Bethlehem so elated. They finally received some good news!

Like the shepherds, we too can live in an anxious state, wondering what bad thing is going to happen next. Sometimes the fear of bad news holds us back from fulfilling our greatest potential. Even though we ought not to obsess over the possibility of bad news, we would do well to learn how to be properly prepared for bad news.

being prepared

The National Geographic channel has several interesting TV shows. One of the shows I find fascinating is called *Doomsday Preppers*. This show explores the lives of otherwise ordinary Americans who are preparing for the end of the world as we know it. Unique in their beliefs, motivations, and strategies, preppers will go to whatever lengths they can to make sure they are prepared for any of life's uncertainties. The preppers are filmed testing the limits of human ingenuity as they develop extreme doomsday survival machines, high-tech shelters, and specialized escape routes.

The good folks on *Doomsday Preppers* may be extremists, but being prepared can be a good thing, especially when it comes to handling bad news.

Within the biblical narrative of Job, we see a man go through some of life's greatest tragedies. Job lost his house, oxen, donkeys, sheep, camels, sons, daughters, and most of his hired hands (Job 1:13–19).

After Job received word about his misfortune, he fell to the ground in worship and said, "Naked I came from my mother's womb, and naked I will depart. The LORD gave and the LORD has taken away; may the name of the LORD be praised" (Job 1:20–21). The text goes on to say, "In all this, Job did not sin by charging God with wrongdoing" (Job 1:22).

What do the doomsday preppers and Job have in common? They both spent time preparing for the worst of the worst. In the core of Job's being, he was prepared to receive bad news, and he didn't let it push him further away from God when it hit home.

Many people struggle to understand life's bad news and respond by casting blame on something or someone. When it seems like there is no one to blame, people tend to blame God.

In our spiritual formation journey, it's good to ask ourselves: If I were Job and all of his misfortune happened to me, would I be able to immediately fall down and praise God?

Of course Job didn't like what had happened, and he would mourn his loss, but his perspective shows us that when bad news hits home, we ought not try to dodge it or slip by it. We ought to prepare for it and embrace it when it happens.

Being prepared for bad news is different from fearing bad news. When we live prepared for bad news, we don't cling to the things of this world or take things for granted. We live as if every moment and every relationship is a gift from God. For we know God is not the orchestrator of bad news. "God is our refuge and strength, an ever-present help in trouble" (Ps. 46:1).

the ultimate purpose

I remember well the moments after my wife showed me her first positive pregnancy test. We were ecstatic. The thought of bringing a child into the world brought us great joy.

Yet I also remember well the moments after she shared with me that she had a miscarriage.

In reference to God's faithful followers, Psalm 112:7–8 says, "They will have no fear of bad news; their hearts are steadfast, trusting in the LORD. Their hearts are secure, they will have no fear; in the end they will look in triumph on their foes."

Here, the psalmist declares that if we make our ultimate purpose in life to obey God, then we have nothing to fear.

Nevertheless, embracing bad news is deeply painful.

In those types of moments our faith is tested to its core. It's easy to follow God's ways when life seems to be going our way, but it's hard to persevere when life seems to be going opposite to the way we planned.

Isn't it interesting that the word *sever* is in the middle of the word perseverance?

In Job's story, we also learn about the core of his character. Job had demonstrated a consistent pattern of faithfulness to God. In reference to Job, God even stated, "There is no one on earth like him, he is blameless and upright, a man who fears God and shuns evil" (Job 1:8). No matter what happened to Job, his heart was fixed on God, and his faith could not be shaken.

In the late nineteenth century, a gentleman named Dr. Payson was overcoming several personal struggles. In a heartfelt moment with several of his friends, he shared these thoughts: "In years gone by, I often dreaded the taking away of certain earthly comforts, but when they have been withdrawn, I have had so much more of the grace and presence of God, that I have had to be thankful for the apparent loss, for it was a real gain. And now that I am a cripple and confined to my house, I am far happier than I ever expected to be, and am as happy as a man could be out of heaven."[2]

These words demonstrate the type of faith Job modeled to others. Regardless of what happened to Job, he knew his ultimate purpose in life was to remain obedient to God. It is precisely because Job knew his purpose that he was able to say to his friends in the midst of his hardships, "Though he slay me, yet will I hope in him; I will surely defend my ways to his face" (Job 13:15).

finding your way out

Bad news has a way of reminding us how fragile life is. We don't know how everything is going to turn out. It may feel like there's

too much to fix or the problem is too large to handle. If you find
yourself feeling crushed under the weight of bad news, take a
moment to breathe. Let go of how it all turns out for a little while,
and allow your Good Shepherd to sweep you off your feet and bring
comfort to your soul. Remember, sometimes the way to getting back
on track is to step off of the track for a moment.

Be assured—God has a plan. A bigger plan than what you can see.

As crazy as it seems, at the end of Job's tragedy, there is triumph.
Throughout his mourning period, Job didn't know what blessings
would be around the corner, but he did know he was committed to
remaining faithful and focused on his ultimate purpose. The text says,

> After Job had prayed for his friends, the LORD restored his for-
> tunes and gave him twice as much as he had before. All his
> brothers and sisters and everyone who had known him before
> came and ate with him in his house. They comforted and
> consoled him over all the trouble the LORD had brought on him,
> and each one gave him a piece of silver and a gold ring.
>
> The LORD blessed the latter part of Job's life more than the
> former part. He had fourteen thousand sheep, six thousand
> camels, a thousand yoke of oxen and a thousand donkeys. And
> he also had seven sons and three daughters. The first daughter
> he named Jemimah, the second Keziah and the third Keren-
> Happuch. Nowhere in all the land were there found women
> as beautiful as Job's daughters, and their father granted them
> an inheritance along with their brothers.
>
> After this, Job lived a hundred and forty years; he saw his
> children and their children to the fourth generation. And so
> Job died, an old man and full of years. (Job 42:10–17)

We have no reason to fear bad news. We don't have to let it hold us back from future blessing. God will prove his faithfulness to us. If we are pursuing God and his purposes in our lives, we have nothing to worry about. Just remember—God is good.

And don't forget, the Lord may want to bless you with a thousand donkeys.

ideas to remember

Bad news is inevitable, but so is God's comfort.
Everything in life, including our life itself, is a gift from God.
Don't think you can avoid bad news; prepare for it.
Our ultimate purpose in life is to obey God.
God is good.

questions to discuss

When have you experienced the fear of bad news?
Have you ever blamed God for something negative in your life?
Without being overly obsessive, like the doomsday preppers, in what ways can you prepare for bad news?
Do you believe you have the inner character which will allow you to persevere and obey God through any situation? Why or why not?
How has God been good to you through situations which may have seemed tragic?

4

when you feel like you've let down God

Fear is the tax that
conscience pays to guilt.

—GEORGE SEWELL

Fear not; you will no longer live in shame.
Don't be afraid; there is no more disgrace for you.
You will no longer remember the shame of your
youth and the sorrows of widowhood.

—ISAIAH 54:4 NLT

Have you ever felt like you let down God? Maybe you blatantly sinned. Maybe you reacted negatively out of stress. Or maybe you honestly didn't know something was wrong.

We all know those feelings of having let down God, don't we? If I were to make a list right now of all the ways I've let down God, it would finish out the rest of this book. In my journey, I am constantly reminded how the only thing I am consistent in is my inconsistency.

My daughter, Jennah, is my princess. Most of the time, she is a splendid child; however, there was a streak in her past where mischief got the best of her. We had just started raising chickens, and they were beginning to lay eggs. Our neighbors, just a stone's throw away, were also raising chickens, but they were getting about three times the amount of eggs we were. I don't know where Jennah gets her competitive edge, but she desperately wanted our neighbors to have fewer eggs and our family to have more.

On one particular evening, Jennah came blasting into the house and boldly announced she had found a bunch of our eggs hidden in the bushes. With excitement in our eyes, we ran outside to scope out this new treasure. Jennah took us right to the bushes and sure enough we saw a pile of six eggs all lumped together. We celebrated our discovery and then took the eggs into the house.

Later in the evening, my wife received a phone call from our neighbors saying they saw Jennah in their pole barn and later noticed that all of their eggs for the day were missing. In no time at all, my wife put two and two together. The eggs Jennah just so happened to discover weren't from our hens!

But now we had a rather significant problem in front of us. Our wonderful child was caught up in an egg scandal. We went into

Jennah's bedroom and asked her where she found the eggs. Hoping she would be honest, we continued to pry. Yet Jennah insisted they were our eggs.

We then shared with her what we knew. After we expounded, her face dropped, and she started to get mad. We asked again, "Jennah, did you take those eggs from the neighbors?"

Finally, Jennah confessed. We then progressed into the disciplinary stages, explaining why we were so disappointed. Not only had she stolen from our neighbors, but she lied to us as well. Jennah was broken and vowed to never do it again.

That should be the end of the story, right? Well, guess what? This "eggscapade" happened two more times. After the third time, we were mad as hornets. We firmly challenged Jennah, "What are you thinking? This is the third time this has happened! How can this be? Why do you continue to take the neighbor's eggs? What gives?"

With tears in her eyes, Jennah replied, "Because I like the feeling I get from taking the eggs."

Ah. I was beginning to see the root of the problem. I knew what Jennah was feeling and could relate. I explained, "Jennah, this can't continue. Will you promise me you won't go and take the neighbor's eggs any longer?"

"I will, Daddy," Jennah exclaimed.

It was an opportunity to teach her about our sinful nature. I shared some of the wrongful things on my life-list that I had to invite God to transform in me. Jennah cried, and we prayed together. And that was that. Up to this day, no more eggs have been stolen!

the good, the bad, and the ugly

As God's children, we have many wonderful moments that please
God, but we also have moments where we disappoint God's heart.
In Romans 7:14–25, the apostle Paul described his heart in this way:

We know that the law is spiritual; but I am unspiritual, sold
as a slave to sin. I do not understand what I do. For what I
want to do I do not do, but what I hate I do. And if I do what
I do not want to do, I agree that the law is good. As it is, it is
no longer I myself who do it, but it is sin living in me. For I
know that good itself does not dwell in me, that is, in my sinful
nature. For I have the desire to do what is good, but I cannot
carry it out. For I do not do the good I want to do, but the evil
I do not want to do—this I keep on doing. Now if I do what
I do not want to do, it is no longer I who do it, but it is sin
living in me that does it.

So I find this law at work: Although I want to do good,
evil is right there with me. For in my inner being I delight in
God's law; but I see another law at work in me, waging war
against the law of my mind and making me a prisoner of the
law of sin at work within me. What a wretched man I am!
Who will rescue me from this body that is subject to death?
Thanks be to God, who delivers me through Jesus Christ our
Lord!

If there is anybody in the Bible I can relate to, it is Paul. I know
exactly what he was talking about. And I also know exactly how he
was delivered from his sinful nature.

When we are honest with ourselves, we recognize an inner fear connected to repeatedly letting down God. The fear of letting down God holds us back from advancing into the people God originally designed us to be. Sometimes we are afraid of even attempting to conquer sin. The result is a life of mediocrity because we fear letting down God again.

Let's face it. We *will* let down God again and again, but what lets down God more is if we don't make an effort to try again. Proverbs 24:16 says, "For though the righteous fall seven times, they rise again."

called higher

Rising again is what disciples of Jesus ought to do best. In Luke 5:1–11, we read about a time when Simon Peter was challenged to rise again:

One day as Jesus was standing by the Lake of Gennesaret; the people were crowding around him and listening to the word of God. He saw at the water's edge two boats, left there by the fishermen, who were washing their nets. He got into one of the boats, the one belonging to Simon, and asked him to put out a little from shore. Then he sat down and taught the people from the boat.

When he had finished speaking, he said to Simon, "Put out into deep water, and let down the nets for a catch."

Simon answered, "Master, we've worked hard all night and haven't caught anything. But because you say so, I will let down the nets."

When they had done so, they caught such a large number of fish that their nets began to break. So they signaled their partners in the other boat to come and help them, and they came and filled both boats so full that they began to sink.

When Simon Peter saw this, he fell at Jesus' knees and said, "Go away from me, Lord; I am a sinful man!" For he and all his companions were astonished at the catch of fish they had taken, and so were James and John, the sons of Zebedee, Simon's partners.

Then Jesus said to Simon, "[Fear not]; from now on you will fish for people." So they pulled their boats up on shore, left everything and followed him.

This is a beautiful story of a disciple overcoming his fear of letting down God. Simon Peter had been out all night fishing. He knew his boat well. He knew his fishing equipment well. And he knew the lake of Gennesaret well. It was just one of those days when the fish had disappeared from their normal holes.

As usual, Jesus was looking for a teachable moment with his disciples. So Jesus told his disciples to put down their nets in the deep waters and watch what happened. Simon Peter thought Jesus' idea was ridiculous. But since Jesus was a well-known rabbi in the land, he did what he said. I can imagine Simon Peter grumbled under his breath as he untangled the nets and dropped them into the water.

Surprisingly, in no time at all, they scored some fish, but not just a few fish—we're talking a boatload! Everyone was astonished.

Afterward, remorse crept over Simon Peter, and he fell at Jesus' feet in the boat pleading, "Go away from me Lord; I am a sinful man."

Simon Peter felt like he let down his rabbi, the Son of God, and he wanted out of the discipleship band. He didn't feel worthy in Jesus' eyes. He felt wretched for his cynicism and doubt. Even more, he thought Jesus would be better off without him around.

Yet Jesus didn't feel the same way. Jesus responded with those two life-changing words—*fear not*. Shockingly, Jesus wanted Simon Peter to step it up and do more. Jesus didn't want Simon Peter to fear letting him down any longer. Jesus wanted Simon Peter to fulfill his greatest potential in life—fishing for people.

Isn't it interesting how Jesus didn't just give Peter a second chance? Instead, Jesus called him higher. In our world today, it's common for people to provide second chances, but the second-chance opportunity usually means they have to start at the back of the line.

In Jesus' second-chance opportunity, he didn't tell Simon Peter to go to the back of the line; he invited him to go to the front of the line! Jesus encouraged Simon Peter to increase his responsibility and advance toward a greater purpose in the world.

The story ends with Simon Peter and the rest of the disciples dropping their nets and following Jesus. The point was made. Jesus knows what he's talking about, he can be trusted, and our wretchedness doesn't limit us from contributing to God's purposes in the world.

dealing with our wretchedness

67

After Simon Peter was proven to be wrong about the fish, he described himself as a sinful man. The Greek word Simon Peter used is *hamartolos*, which doesn't just mean sinful; it means pre-eminently sinful! Simon Peter was linking himself with the worst of society, namely, the tax collectors, prostitutes, and heathens.[1]

Take note, at this point in Simon Peter's journey, he would not have heard the stories recounted in Luke 14: the parables of the lost sheep, lost coin, and lost son, all of which deal specifically with God's reenergizing grace. Simon Peter wasn't aware of God's unconditional love, and as a result, he described himself as *harmartolos* and was immobilized by the fear of letting down his rabbi.

In speaking about morals, Ernest Hemingway reportedly once said, "I know only that what is moral is what you feel good after and what is immoral is what you feel bad after." This is a popular view of sin. Many have lived by this philosophy, including Simon Peter. However, Jesus would not have defined sin in that way. For Jesus, sin was an attitude of wanting your way instead of God's way. How we subjectively feel about an action afterward is irrelevant. Remember my daughter's egg-stealing experience? Sin can feel really good afterward!

Simon Peter obviously felt bad about his attitude and actions. He felt great remorse and considered himself unworthy to be around Jesus. Hence he told Jesus to go away.

An immature view of sin fueled Simon Peter's fear of letting down his rabbi. There are two all-too-common inadequate views of sin: Some people don't really believe they have sinned, and others don't believe they can be forgiven. Simon Peter was one of those who didn't believe he could be forgiven; he was too *harmartolos*.

To be sure, our sinfulness matters to God. God cannot tolerate sin. In Habakkuk 1:13, the prophet said, "Your eyes are too pure to look on evil; you cannot tolerate wrongdoing."

Whenever we do sin, God's Spirit in us is grieved, which is why we feel guilty afterward. When we choose to give in to temptation, we are choosing in that moment to live apart from God's will for our lives. This doesn't cause God to hate us. God still loves us. But our choice pains God's heart.

As demonstrated by Jesus and Simon Peter's ongoing relationship, sin does not affect God's eternal relationship with us, which was established when we trusted in Christ's payment for our sins. When we sin, we might feel like we are the worst of the worst, but God looks past our sin and sees Christ within. Only because God sees Christ in us can we be re-empowered to follow God and desire sin no more.

God's amazing grace doesn't merely overlook sin—it overthrows sin.

Let's be clear though, our desire to sin affects our communication with God and our usefulness in his plans. Sin dulls us to the things God wants us to be thinking about and doing.

In Psalm 32:3–5, the great King David said, "When I kept silent, my bones wasted away through my groaning all day long. For day and night your hand was heavy on me; my strength was sapped as in the heat of summer. Then I acknowledged my sin to you and did not cover up my iniquity. I said, 'I will confess my transgressions to the LORD.' And you forgave the guilt of my sin."

King David presented us with the proper response to our sinfulness. King David didn't deny his sin. He didn't remain preoccupied with it. He simply confessed it, experienced freedom, and advanced.

doing a 180

In my daughter's scandalous egg story, there was a moment when my wife and I fully knew what she had done. Yet my daughter was unable to confess the truth about what happened.

It is important to know what genuine confession is. In its simplest form, confession means to agree with God.

Just like my wife and I already knew what my daughter had done, God also already knows what we've done. So we might as well be honest and agree with him!

The author of 1 John 1:9 said it plainly, "If we confess our sins, he is faithful and just and will forgive us our sins and purify us from all unrighteousness."

Confession doesn't mean begging God for forgiveness. Jesus already gave us all the forgiveness we'll ever need when he was hanging on the cross and uttered the words, "It is finished" (John 19:30). Confession means freely admitting our sin and being willing to take the first step toward repentance.

To be sure, confession isn't the end-all. Confession is the beginning of all. After confession comes repentance, which essentially means desiring to do a 180, turning away from those sinful desires and fully following Jesus. Repenting is the active movement back toward God propelled by his grace.

After we experience the transformation of repentance, like Simon Peter, we can get up off our knees, leave our nets, and follow Jesus, with a deeper desire to obey his commands.

lingering guilt

I'll be honest, I've sinned enough to know that we can still feel guilty even after we have confessed and repented of our sin. At times, I have even thought it seemed spiritual to beat up myself after I sinned. I believed if I lowered my perception of myself, my humility would please God. However, that couldn't be further from the truth.

God doesn't want us to belittle ourselves; God wants us to be ourselves. Part of the confession and repentance process is praising God for the fact that all of our sins have been paid for by Christ. On that basis only, God says, "For I will forgive their wickedness and will remember their sins no more" (Heb. 8:12).

When we praise God, we act in faith and respond to God's truth about us instead of relying upon how we feel. When we feel like we need to belittle and beat up ourselves over our past record, we are essentially focusing on our sin rather than on Christ and his forgiveness. In other words, we are giving the Evil One the glory instead of rejoicing in Christ's victory over sin and death.

Remember, "There is now no condemnation for those who are in Christ Jesus" (Rom. 8:1).

becoming more

Many people saw steam raise the lid of a kettle, but only James Watt went on to think of a steam engine.

God looks at us in the same way Mr. Watt looked at the potential energy from a steaming kettle. He sees what we can or will be, not just what we are. But God also sees us attaining new levels of freedom from sin and guilt. God longs to turn us into a useful steam engine, transforming the world around us.

Simon Peter didn't know it at the time, but one of his most positive qualities was his willingness to try again. Even though he was tired, doubtful, and perhaps thought Jesus was foolish, he obeyed Jesus and tried dropping his nets one more time.

For many people, the disaster of life is that they gave up just one effort too soon.

We never know where God is going to take us, but we can trust it will be good, and we don't ever need to fear letting him down along the way.

When we fall down, Jesus only asks us to become more.

ideas to remember

God doesn't define us by our sin; he sees our potential to overcome sin.

Rising again is what disciples of Jesus ought to do best.

Some people don't believe they have sinned; others don't believe they are forgiven.

Don't deny or become preoccupied with sin; simply confess it and move forward in God's grace.

Repentance is active movement back toward God propelled by his grace.

questions to discuss

Have you ever felt like you let down God?

Did you allow your wrongdoings to push God away or to propel you forward in grace?

Do you struggle with accepting Christ's forgiveness for your past, present, and future?

How can confession of sin empower you to overcome sin?

Where do you see God taking you in the future?

5

when you
don't believe

Give me one hundred preachers who fear nothing
but sin and desire nothing but God, and I care not
whether they be clergymen or laymen, they
alone will shake the gates of hell and set
up the kingdom of heaven upon earth.

—JOHN WESLEY

I do believe; help me
overcome my unbelief!

—MARK 9:24

I recently had a wiring problem with the taillights on my vehicle. My lights would randomly turn on and off. I knew I needed to fix the problem; however, I was in a busy phase and didn't want to take the time to diagnose the cause. One evening, as I was out and about, a police officer crept up behind me and tailed me for several miles.

Just before I was about to pull into my destination, the lights and sirens flicked on. My heart dropped and a wretched sinking feeling saturated my body. The police officer made his way to my window and asked me the dreaded question, "Do you know why I pulled you over?"

Confidently, I stated, "Well, it probably has something to do with my taillights. I know they are out. I'm working on trying to get them fixed."

The officer didn't look satisfied. He quickly continued, "Not only are your taillights out, but you were swerving all over the road! I have it all on video if you'd like to see it. I need to see your license and registration."

I fumbled around my console trying to find my identification. Eventually, I found it and gave it to him, and then he promptly walked back to his car. It looked like he was checking out a few things, but it didn't take long before he was back at my window.

The officer said, "Mr. Love, have you been drinking tonight?"

"No sir," I said.

He responded, "Are you sure? It's best if you be honest with me and tell me now."

"No, I promise. I have not been drinking!" I said.

With a little gruffness in his voice, the officer said, "Well, I'm going to need you to blow into this."

The officer held up a breathalyzer contraption. I pulled back and said, "Whoa, you really don't believe me?"

"Mr. Love, I need you to breathe into this," he affirmed.

Not wanting to make a scene, I complied and gave it a solid blow. After studying his breathalyzer for a moment he said, "Hmm. You weren't lying. Well, good for you!"

I quickly responded, "I'm a pastor. I wouldn't lie to you."

I'm not sure if the pastoral reference helped, but the officer chuckled a little. He proceeded to give me a fix-it ticket for my lights and told me God would want me to stay within the lines. No lie!

I drove off content, but a little bit confounded. Little did the officer know, but I take extra strides in life to be honest. It didn't feel good to not be believed in.

Maybe that's how God feels when we struggle to believe his words.

choosing to believe

There are times in our lives when we believe God wholeheartedly. God could ask us to move to Ethiopia, and we would move. Yet there are other times in life when we struggle to believe anything God has to say.

In Luke 8:40–56, there is a story about a man who overcame his fear of believing Jesus' words. Here is that moving story:

Now when Jesus returned, a crowd welcomed him, for they were all expecting him. Then a man named Jairus, a synagogue leader, came and fell at Jesus' feet, pleading with him to come to his house because his only daughter, a girl of about twelve, was dying.

As Jesus was on his way, the crowds almost crushed him. And a woman was there who had been subject to bleeding for twelve years, but no one could heal her. She came up behind him and touched the edge of his cloak, and immediately her bleeding stopped.

"Who touched me?" Jesus asked.

When they all denied it, Peter said, "Master, the people are crowding and pressing against you."

But Jesus said, "Someone touched me; I know that power has gone out from me."

Then the woman, seeing that she could not go unnoticed, came trembling and fell at his feet. In the presence of all the people, she told why she had touched him and how she had been instantly healed. Then he said to her, "Daughter, your faith has healed you. Go in peace."

While Jesus was still speaking, someone came from the house of Jairus, the synagogue leader. "Your daughter is dead," he said. "Don't bother the teacher anymore."

Hearing this, Jesus said to Jairus, "[Fear not]; just believe, and she will be healed."

When he arrived at the house of Jairus, he did not let anyone go in with him except Peter, John and James, and the child's father and mother. Meanwhile, all the people were wailing and mourning for her. "Stop wailing," Jesus said. "She is not dead but asleep."

They laughed at him, knowing that she was dead. But he took her by the hand and said, "My child, get up!" Her spirit returned, and at once she stood up. Then Jesus told them to give her something to eat. Her parents were astonished, but he ordered them not to tell anyone what had happened.

There are many interesting components to this story. Jairus was greatly concerned about his twelve-year-old daughter because she seemed near death. Jairus had most likely heard a few of the stories circulating around the community about healings this man Jesus supposedly had been performing. Deciding to take the stories at face value, and desperate to save his daughter, Jairus ran to Jesus and pleaded for him to come and heal his daughter.

Because Jairus was the leader of the local Jewish synagogue, he would have been considered a man of great faith. Being a synagogue leader meant he was well-respected in the community, and he probably had a good amount of wealth. He may have felt as if life had given him many things but was about to take away the most precious thing.

As Jairus and Jesus started toward his house, a woman who had an issue of bleeding for twelve years reached out and touched Jesus, believing she could be healed. Sure enough, she was healed right there on the spot. Jairus would have been right by Jesus' side and witnessed this miraculous event.

After Jesus took care of the woman, someone from Jairus's home met them on the road, proclaiming his little girl had died. Jesus was too late to the scene. We can imagine Jairus's eyes closing as sadness crept over his face. But then Jesus turned to him and said, "Fear not; just believe, for your daughter will be healed."

In this moment, Jairus had a choice. Should he believe in Jesus? Or should he scrap his Jesus idea and enter into a time of mourning?

Despite Jairus's feelings, he chose to stick by Jesus' side and took him into his daughter's room. When he arrived, people were wailing at the loss of this girl.

Jesus' reply? "Stop it!"

It turns out Jairus's little girl was not dead; she was simply in a nonresponsive state. What great news! And to think, she would have been buried alive if Jesus had not come onto the scene. Jesus may not have raised her from the dead, but he certainly did give her life back to her.

Jesus stepped in and completely redefined the situation for everyone in Jairus's household, turning screeching sorrow into songs of hope.

Jairus is a splendid example of a man who had a choice to believe or not believe. Jairus overcame his fears and chose to believe. When all hope seemed lost—he chose to believe. When the path of healing didn't make sense—he chose to believe. And when everyone else had given up—he chose to believe.

going the right way

On a recent anniversary excursion with my wife, we decided to go paddleboating on a nearby lake. We snapped on our life vests, unhooked the boat from the dock, and pushed off into the sparkling waters. It didn't take long to notice something was wrong with the paddleboat. Apparently, the rudder was stuck, and we could only go to the right. We probably looked like two romantic idiots out there circling around and around. We eventually made it back to the dock, which took some skill, and switched to another paddleboat.

Our sense of belief is kind of like a rudder on a paddleboat. It steers us in the right direction. If we believe God will supply our needs, then we will head in that direction. If we are afraid we won't have enough to live on, then we will go in that direction. What we believe is the direction we will travel.

When my wife and I were first married, I was the student ministries pastor at a very strong church. I loved being a youth pastor. At age twenty-two, I was already entrenched in my dream job. Everything was going wonderfully. The ministry was expanding. Lives were changing. I couldn't have been more content. That is, until I attended a motivational church leadership conference.

At some point during one of the worship sessions, I was pinned to my seat by the Spirit of God. I knew God was doing some character work in me, but I didn't know he was also doing some calling work too. As I sat with my hands clenched around my head, I sensed the Lord prompting me to pursue being a lead pastor.

My initial response was, "No way, Lord! I can't lead a church. I can't lead adults. I'm not a good teacher. I'm too young." Yet my excuses didn't seem to matter. I knew the Lord had called me, but I didn't want to believe that I was to be a leader in the church. To believe God meant I would be required to leave my safe environment.

Looking back now, I can see the Lord's hand at work in my life. Those promptings at the conference weren't just my latest ideas for my life; they were words from the Lord.

After hearing the Lord's words, I knew I had a choice. Would I choose to stay in my comfortable role or would I choose to be like Jairus and just believe?

leaving comfort zones

When you go to a restaurant, do you usually order the same type of meal or do you try something unique? I typically order what I know is good. I don't like to waste money, so I want to make sure the meal is going to be well worth it.

Humans are creatures of habit. We usually prefer to do what we know will make us feel good. When it comes to following God's direction, we will always feel tension. Remember, God wants us to pursue courage, not comfort. Many times, the only way we will ever grow spiritually is if we leave our comfort zones. It is the only way we will develop new skills. It is the only way we will build new relational networks. And it is the only way we will impact lives for God.

In the biblical narrative, most of the great stories of our faith ancestors began with them being required to leave their comfort zones.

Abraham had to leave his father's house and journey to an unknown territory which the Lord would reveal to him when he arrived there (see Gen. 12:1).

Moses had to leave the comforts of his home in Midian to fulfill his calling to free his people (see Ex. 3:10).

David, as a young lad, was required to take down a Philistine giant one rock at a time (see 1 Sam. 17:32).

The list could go on and on. Every story of great faith begins with an individual stepping out of his or her comfort zone.

When we try something new, we don't know exactly how it will turn out. We cannot possibly plan for everything that will come our way. However, we must trust in the ultimate destination. Without a deep sense of trust in the end result, we will hinder ourselves from the get-go. We might even miss the spiritual fortitude necessary to overcome the inevitable obstacles along the way.

It's not easy to leave our comfort zones. We can always come up with really good excuses to not believe God's words. We can always play it safe. And we can always cling too tightly to life.

releasing control

Have you ever seen the bumper sticker that reads, "God is my copilot"? This idea of God being our copilot seems nice, but have you ever thought about what this saying really means? In an airplane, there is a pilot and a copilot. For God to be my copilot means that I, as the primary pilot, am the one calling the shots. God's not in control; I'm in control. Now that's a scary thought! I know myself well enough to know if I'm in control of the plane, we're going to crash and burn.

Since the days of Adam and Eve, humanity has struggled with being in control. We want to direct the outcome of situations and events toward our preferred preferences, so we cling, contrive, and control.

Jesus talked a lot about releasing control and letting go of our selfish desires. In Matthew 10:39, Jesus said, "Whoever finds their life will lose it, and whoever loses their life for my sake will find it." Kind of a puzzling thought, isn't it? Jesus didn't mean we need to relinquish our responsibilities. He didn't mean we should give up our duties in life. What Jesus was referring to is a person's willingness to live selflessly.

All too often, we tend to view relationships for what we can get from them, instead of what we can give to them. When we hold so tightly to the pursuit of worldly things, we will inevitably lose the very heart of who we are. Even worse, if our life is all about accomplishing our agenda, then we will eventually end up manipulating the people around us.

As we follow Jesus' way, he invites us to rediscover the core of our being. According to Jesus, true life will only come as we pursue selflessness. Then, and only then, will we be able to do what God asks of us.

blind faith

Years ago, when John D. Rockefeller was running a gigantic empire known as the Standard Oil Company, one of the employees made a disastrous decision, which cost the company more than two million dollars. Fear swept through the company as everyone expected Rockefeller not only to fire the man responsible, but to erupt in anger as well.

Edward T. Bedford, a partner in the company, was scheduled to see Rockefeller. As he entered his office he saw this powerful man bent over his desk busily writing on a pad of paper. Bedford stood silently, not wishing to interrupt. After a few minutes, Rockefeller looked up. "Oh, it's you, Bedford. I suppose you've heard about our loss. I've been thinking it over and have been making some notes."

Bedford later told the story this way: "Across the top of the page was written, 'Points in favor of Mr. _____.' And there, underneath the title, was a long list of the man's virtues, including a brief description of how he had helped the company make the right decision on three separate occasions—decisions that had earned the company many times the cost of his recent error."

Surprisingly, the man kept his job. Bedford left the meeting forever changed in how he viewed other employees of the company.[1]

Let's be honest, sometimes we don't believe God's words. Sometimes we goof and go our own way for an extended period of time. I know I have. Nevertheless, there is no better time to go back to God than right now.

Thankfully, our God looks at us like Rockefeller looked at his flawed employee. God doesn't zoom in on our mistakes; God zooms out and sees our future potential.

Maybe God has spoken to you in the past and you decided not to listen to him because you feared the implications of believing his words. Maybe that's your story.

You might feel like Abraham in Genesis 12:1 when God said, "Go. . . to the land I will show you." Talk about blind faith! If you follow God long enough, there will come a time when blind faith is all you're going to have. All the human reasoning around you will tell you God can't possibly do what he has promised you. In this moment, you'll be left to make a choice. Do you believe God, or do you believe only in what you can see, handle, and measure?

In his book *Lion and Lamb*, Brennan Manning recounts an incident that took place when a two-story house caught on fire. The family was making their way out of the house when the smallest boy became terrified, tore away from his mother, and ran back upstairs. Suddenly, he appeared at a smoke-filled window crying hysterically. Standing outside, his father shouted, "Jump, son! Jump! I'll catch you."

The boy cried, "But Daddy, I can't see you."

"I know," his father called, "but I can see you."[2]

Throughout God's entire storybook, not one of God's faithful saints was able to see how it would all turn out in advance.

The same is true for us. But we can trust our heavenly Father's voice to lead us in the right direction.

ideas to remember

God doesn't force us to believe; he simply gives us the choice to believe.

What we believe will determine the direction we travel.

Stories of great faith begin with individuals stepping out of their comfort zones.

Releasing control isn't about relinquishing responsibility; it's about becoming selfless.

Our heavenly Father's voice can be trusted.

questions to discuss

Do you struggle to believe God's words? Why?

When was a time where you chose not to believe God's words? What happened?

When was a time you chose to believe God's words? What happened?

Is it difficult for you to step out of your comfort zone? Why?

Have you ever acted as if God was your copilot? What was the result?

Why is releasing control difficult for us?

In what areas of your life do you need to believe God's words to you?

6

when you are
worried about being
deprived

Where does your security lie? Is God your refuge,
your hiding place, your stronghold, your shepherd,
your counselor, your friend, your redeemer, your
savior, your guide? If he is, you don't need
to search any further for security.

—ELISABETH ELLIOT

But even if you suffer for doing what is right,
God will reward you for it. So don't
worry or be afraid of their threats.

—1 PETER 3:14 NLT

Have you ever wondered if God really cares about you? Have you ever feared being deprived of your daily needs?

Sometimes we don't take great faith risks because we wonder if God will provide for our needs.

Take a moment and absorb the insightful lyrics of Frank E. Graeff's hymn called, "Does My Savior Care?"

> Does Jesus care when my heart is pained
> Too deeply for mirth or song,
> As the burdens press, and the cares distress,
> And the way grows weary and long?
> Does Jesus care when my way is dark
> With a nameless dread and fear?
> As the daylight fades into deep night shades,
> Does he care enough to be near?
> Does Jesus care when I've said "good-bye"
> To the dearest on earth to me,
> And my sad heart aches till it nearly breaks —
> Is it aught to him? Does he see?
> Oh yes, he cares, I know he cares,
> His heart is touched with my grief;
> When the days are weary, the long nights dreary,
> I know my Savior cares.[1]

When it comes to the big concerns in life, I have no doubt my Savior cares. However, I struggle when it comes to the small things in life.

What would it look like if we didn't have to fear being deprived? What if we could trust God to be there for us in both the big concerns and the little concerns of life?

We might just find we'd be willing to step into greater levels of faith.

not forgotten

In Luke 12, we see Jesus using an ancient Jewish teaching practice called *charez*, which means "stringing pearls." In verses 6–7, Jesus strings together several pearls of wisdom in regards to how much God cares for his creation. Here is Jesus' *charez*: "Are not five sparrows sold for two pennies? Yet not one of them is forgotten by God. Indeed, the very hairs of your head are all numbered. [Fear not]; you are worth more than many sparrows."

Here we see Jesus expounding on God's great concern for us, even in the details of life. To God we are never lost in the crowd. Even the sparrow has value.

Someone once calculated the hairs on people's heads. They discovered a blonde has about 145,000 hairs; a brunette has about 120,000; and a red head has, 90,000.[2] This person had way too much time on their hands!

At some point in our relationship with God, we need to embrace God's detailed care for us. We are not just a number. We are not just a cause. We are a valued possession of God.

Be assured: God didn't create us only to watch us crash. God promised to be with us through everything. In fact, God's "withness" is the most common promise found in the Scriptures.

leave your burdens

My house was built in the middle of an open meadow. I happen to love trees and had always dreamed of a home surrounded by prickly pines. Last year I decided to make my dream come true, so I set out to plant infant pines all around my house. Since I decided to plant the pines in the middle of summer, I needed to water them every day. The trees were planted farther away than what my garden hose could reach, so my best idea was to fill up a five-gallon bucket and take the water to them. Day after day, I made trip after trip, carrying those five-gallon buckets. Seriously—I have never been so sore in my life!

Sometimes, we carry our burdens around as if they are five-gallon buckets attached to our arms. Our bodies were never meant to carry around that kind of weight. We may not fully realize it, but often we are spiritually sore from the burdens we carry.

We might feel like life is overwhelming. It brings so many demands—relationally, financially, and occupationally. We can quickly slip into a worldview which doesn't include much involvement from God. It's easy to feel like our future is self-made and God doesn't care about our burdens. Or worse yet, God doesn't have time to deal with our burdens.

The author of 1 Peter 5:7 was quick to remind us, "Cast all your anxiety on him because he cares for you." We can be confident in God's ability to take our burdens. But we also must find the confidence to leave our burdens with him.

Pouring out our souls before the Lord is our first step in leaving our burdens. Every burden, every fear, every emotion in our bucket must come out. If we are going to live fearless lives, our burden bucket must be bone dry.

Psalm 62:8 says, "Trust in him at all times, you people; pour out your hearts to him, for God is our refuge."

Pouring out our hearts involves a struggle during which our deepest emotions and needs flow out of us and into God's hands. We might refer to this as "spilling your guts." This is when we are completely honest and authentic before God.

In another psalm, the lyricist poured out his heart before the Lord in this way: "Hear my prayer, LORD; let my cry for help come to you. Do not hide your face from me when I am in distress. Turn your ear to me; when I call, answer me quickly. For my days vanish like smoke; my bones burn like glowing embers. My heart is blighted and withered like grass; I forget to eat my food" (Ps. 102:1–4).

It's freeing to know we can be completely raw and authentic before the Lord. We don't have to sugarcoat our words. Believe it or not, God wants us to be honest with him. That's the only way we can truly receive God's help.

In Psalm 62:8, notice that something comes before we are to pour out our heart. The psalmist makes sure to emphasize this simple but profound phrase: Trust in God at *all* times.

Isn't it true that if we are going to pour out our heart to someone, they must be someone we can trust? God wants us to know he can be trusted with whatever is on our heart, even if what is on our heart is our confusion with the way God works. God is the most trustworthy friend we could ever have and he will carry us through any fearful situation.

carry on

It's a daily struggle to empty our burden bucket, but God desperately wants us to live free. In fact, this type of freedom is the essence of heaven.

In churches, we hear a lot about the way into heaven, but we probably don't hear as much as we should about how to get heaven into earth. In the Lord's Prayer, Jesus clearly laid out his vision of heaven on earth. In Matthew 6:10, Jesus prayed, "Your kingdom come, your will be done, on earth as it is in heaven." When Jesus spoke about God's coming kingdom, he was talking about our earthly experience of heaven.

The world is desperate to know how to live on earth as if it were heaven. When people see someone living free of their burdens and carrying on, they are inspired to believe in God.

Recently, I met a man named Mr. Applebee in a coffee shop. As he adjusted his suspenders, Mr. Applebee struck up a conversation with me and proceeded to tell me his life story and why he shouldn't be alive. He was in a tragic accident and suffered a severe head wound which left him in a coma. When he woke up, the doctors shared with him what he had been though over the previous several months. Without a moment's pause, he looked up and said, "Now God, I praise you. You spared my life and now I give it back to you. For the rest of my days I will be your servant."

After years of rehabilitation, Mr. Applebee went on to obtain a masters degree in psychology, with an emphasis on substance abuse counseling. Then he started a ministry that reaches the brokenhearted and addicted. At every opportunity, he shares with his clients the life change he found through Jesus Christ.

It boggles my mind to know about a man with a story like Mr. Applebee's. He was able to take a destructive event and allow it to be used to advance God's purposes in the world.

continued service

Life may have beaten us down and kicked us around, but we can still be useful in God's kingdom work. Romans 8:28 says, "And we know that in all things God works for the good of those who love him, who have been called according to his purpose." This verse is a promise. We can have certainty from the promise. We can experience completeness from the promise. And we can know contentment from the promise.

God is like a junkyard artist; he likes to take messes and make masterpieces. Those who love God don't need to fear being deprived because God will always care for us and use our broken story for something good.

In his book *God in the Dock*, C. S. Lewis wrote, "In Hamlet a branch breaks and Ophelia is drowned. Did she die because the branch broke or because Shakespeare wanted her to die at that point in the play? Either—both—whichever you please. The alternative suggested by the question is not a real alternative at all—once you have grasped how Shakespeare is making the whole play."[3]

In all of Shakespeare's works, he is the chief orchestrator, the sovereign playwright. He directs the outcome and uses whatever means he desires. To be sure, God is more sovereign than Shakespeare. But like Shakespeare, God uses all kinds of things and events for his good purposes in the world.

Imagine what God might use in your life.

Our burdens shouldn't hold us back from fulfilling our greatest potential. They should push us forward.

We never have to fear being deprived or wonder if God is going to resurrect us.

Resurrecting is what God does best.

ideas to remember

God cares about the details in our life.

God is committed to being there for us.

God desires to free us from life's burdens.

No matter what has happened to us, we must carry on and fulfill God's purposes.

God likes to turn messes into masterpieces.

questions to discuss

Why do you think we struggle to believe God cares about us?

Why do you think God's most common promise in Scripture is to be with us?

Do you have any burdens you need to lay down before the cross of Christ? If so, which ones?

What messes in your life has God already turned into a beautiful masterpiece?

What messes in your life do you need to ask God to turn into a masterpiece?

What would it look like if you didn't fear being deprived and stepped out in great faith?

7

when salvation
seems
questionable

Courage is almost a contradiction in terms.
It means a strong desire to live, taking
the form of a readiness to die.

—G. K. CHESTERTON

In God, whose word I praise—
in God I trust and am not afraid.
What can mere mortals do to me?

—PSALM 56:4

The drama began after the mother put her three kids to bed. At about 9:30 she noticed flames on the patio and quickly called 9-1-1. Then came the explosion—flames ignited a propane tank, and the blast sent smoke and flames into the home.

The mother sprinted inside to rush her three-year-old girl out the front door and into the hands of neighbors. Then she hurried back, grabbed her fifteen-month-old girl, and then dashed back a third time through the thick smoke to rescue her six-year-old boy. She managed to get all of her children out of the house just as the fire crew arrived. One of the crew that night was her husband, a fireman who arrived to find his family safe, thanks his wife's heroics.[1]

Life-saving rescue operations are a staple of storytelling, and they are stories worth telling. They highlight a cast of people on two sides: the heroes and those in danger, needing to be saved.

It could be said that the entire story of God is the account of one great rescue operation for all humanity. At the turn of the first century, the hero (Jesus) enters the scene and those in danger (us) are saved. Yet for much of God's history, God's people were stuck, waiting and wondering if God was going to save them.

the coming King

In John 12:12–19, we witness the moment where God broke through the silence and clearly defined Jesus as the great rescuer that God's people were anticipating. Here is the striking story:

The next day the great crowd that had come for the festival heard that Jesus was on his way to Jerusalem. They took palm branches and went out to meet him, shouting,

"Hosanna!"

"Blessed is he who comes in the name of the Lord!"

"Blessed is the king of Israel!"

Jesus found a young donkey and sat on it, as it is written:

"[Fear not], Daughter Zion; see, your king is coming, seated on a donkey's colt."

At first his disciples did not understand all this. Only after Jesus was glorified did they realize that these things had been written about him and that these things had been done to him.

Now the crowd that was with him when he called Lazarus from the tomb and raised him from the dead continued to spread the word. Many people, because they had heard that he had performed this sign, went out to meet him. So the Pharisees said to one another, "See, this is getting us nowhere. Look how the whole world has gone after him!"

This event, which is typically the focus of the week before Easter, took place just before the Jewish festival of Passover. Passover was a huge celebration. Jews from all around the region would swarm Jerusalem like bees around a hive.

News and rumors had gone out that Jesus, the man who had performed great miracles, was on his way to Jerusalem. It is estimated that more than two million people may have been in Jerusalem at the time of Jesus' great reception.[2]

The people who awaited Jesus' arrival were poised and ready to receive Jesus as a mighty conqueror. They greeted him with the phrase, "Hosanna! Blessed is he who comes in the name of the Lord!" Take note, *hosanna* is a strong Hebrew word meaning "save now!"

Even more, this greeting was a very popular quotation derived from Psalm 118:25–26, which was a significant reference to God's salvation plan. Without a doubt, when the people were chanting the words of this psalm, they were looking at Jesus as their great Savior, their hero.

In such a crowded and loud setting, it was impossible for Jesus to speak to the people. His voice could not have reached the masses. So he did something for all to see. He rode into the city on a donkey's colt.

In dramatic fashion, Jesus was acting out the words Zechariah the prophet had used many years earlier in speaking of the coming savior. Notice that the quote from Zechariah 9:9 begins with those two life-changing words—*fear not*. There was no need for the people to fear, because God, the great rescuer, was on the way.

In this donkey-riding event, Jesus was also claiming to be a particular kind of savior, with a particular kind of agenda. When kings rode into cities on horses, they were stirring up images of war. Yet when kings rode in on donkeys, they were rousing images of peace.

Judging by the response of the Pharisees, Jesus was exactly who God's people were waiting for.

wrestling in waiting

We spend a lot of time waiting. We wait in lines for things like purchasing groceries, being seated at a restaurant, being attended to at a bank, seeing a film, and getting into an amusement park. Statisticians say the average person ends up waiting sixty-two minutes a day—which is three years or 4.3 percent of a person's life.

Most people aren't big fans of waiting. I don't know anyone who enjoys the process. Waiting is simply an inevitable part of life's journey, including our faith journey. All throughout the biblical narrative, we see God's people waiting for him.

In the book of Jeremiah, a prophetic book written around the early sixth century B.C., there is a popular verse which receives a lot of attention. At first glance, it seems extremely uplifting. The verse is found in Jeremiah 29:11 and reads, "'For I know the plans I have for you,' declares the LORD, 'plans to prosper you and not to harm you, plans to give you hope and a future!'" Sound familiar?

I will admit, Jeremiah 29:11 is a lovely hope-filled verse, and it does preach well, but have you ever noticed the broader context? The verse preceding Jeremiah 29:11 reveals something unique about the way God tends to work. Jeremiah 29:10 states, "This is what the LORD says: 'When seventy years are completed for Babylon, I will come to you and fulfill my good promise to bring you back to this place [their homeland].'"

Isn't that interesting? God will come for his people and give them a new future in seventy years! So what were God's people supposed to do in the meantime? Just wait around?

Exactly.

Imagine hearing Jeremiah's prophetic words for the first time—especially if you were already older. What would you have been thinking? If you knew you might not be alive when God's promises were going to be fulfilled, what would be your motivation for living? Wouldn't you question God's salvation plan? Wouldn't you ask, "Why not right now God? Now is when we need saving! Can't you see us in our oppression and suffering?"

As generations continued to pass on, we can imagine it seemed like God's salvation was becoming more and more questionable. Many people were beginning to lose hope. In fact, the reason we have the prophetic books in the Bible is precisely because God's people needed to hear a voice calling them to stay faithful, to stay the course, because God's salvation was on the way.

Hundreds of years before Jesus' triumphal entry, the Jewish people were living in great anticipation, expecting God to intervene in history and save them through an earthly ruler, a king. Many people wrongfully assumed this king would conquer the Roman oppressors and set up his reign on earth. Indeed, God's plan was entirely earth-centered, but not the type of plan that involved a physical ruler and physical kingdom.

We can understand why the people were so antsy for their savior. Talk about who this savior would be and where he would come from was just a part of the day-to-day Jewish culture.

Even more, before Jesus, there were many wannabe messiahs who attempted to orchestrate messianic movements, but none lasted. By the time Jesus came onto the scene, the people were ready. They had waited long enough and were thrilled to their core that God had chosen their generation to usher in his kingdom strategy.

The big struggle for those who followed Jesus, including his closest disciples, was embracing the reality that Jesus wasn't setting up an earthly empire. He was orchestrating a life-changing, invisible spiritual kingdom.

In John 18:36, Jesus said, "My kingdom is not of this world. If it were, my servants would fight to prevent my arrest by the Jewish leaders. But now my kingdom is from another place." For whatever reason, Jesus' disciples didn't understand what he meant by this invisible kingdom until well after he died and rose again.

Clearly, Jesus wanted to see the values of heaven enter earth. But why do we struggle to live in that truth? Are we afraid of embracing the implications? Are we afraid of making the deep changes necessary to see this vision fulfilled? What might change in our lives if we truly embraced heaven as a realm on earth?

let it shine

When I was preparing to get hitched, Emily and I went through a series of intense marriage counseling sessions with a respected Christian counselor. Week after week, we were confronted with the blind spots in our lives. I would have preferred visits to the dentist over seeing our counselor. It was as painful as a root canal. But definitely needed!

After a few sessions and a few sharp arguments, I became acutely aware of a problem with pride in my life. Up until those marriage counseling sessions, I was the most humble person I knew! However, I was beginning to discover that if Emily and I were going make it in marriage, I needed to deal with my pride.

One day I shared this realization with a mentor of mine. He wisely recommended I take six months and make my one prayer: "Lord, live in me, and let your humility shine through me." It seemed like a good idea, so I agreed to bask in this prayer.

I grew up in the WWJD era. It seemed like every Christian I knew had either a bracelet or a charm that said WWJD. The idea was, if people asked, "What would Jesus do?" about everything in life, then they could live holy and right with God. At the time, I wasn't very astute in theology, so it seemed like a good idea. However, when I started to pray this prayer of humility, I began to realize I wasn't asking WWJD. I was pursuing something much deeper. I wasn't trying to replicate Jesus—I was attempting to let Jesus live in me and shine forth from within.

This shift rocked my world. I wasn't just attempting to replicate Jesus' humility. I was embracing the fact that the Holy Spirit entered my body when I accepted Jesus into my life, and I was opening myself up to allow God to shine through me. It wasn't overnight, but deep inner change began to happen, and Emily noticed something different about me. I still had my glitches and misses, to be sure, but my heart was morphing. I was experiencing heaven on earth. God's earthly sense of salvation was beginning to feel real, as Christ was living through me.

In 1920 Harry Dixon Loes wrote one of the most famous children's gospel songs. The song was most likely derived from Matthew 5:14–16 which says, "You are the light of the world. A town built on a hill cannot be hidden. Neither do people light a lamp and put it under a bowl. Instead they put it on its stand, and it gives light to everyone in the house. In the same way, let your light shine before others, that they may see your good deeds and glorify your Father in heaven."

Here are those special lyrics. Sing it out loud if you know it.

> This little light of mine, I'm gonna let it shine.
> This little light of mine, I'm gonna let it shine.
> This little light of mine, I'm gonna let it shine.
> Let it shine, let it shine, let it shine.

> Won't let Satan blow it out, I'm gonna let it shine.
> Won't let Satan blow it out, I'm gonna let it shine.
> Won't let Satan blow it out, I'm gonna let it shine.
> Let it shine, let it shine, let it shine.

We would do well to sing this song every day, wouldn't we?

singing theology

Many singers and lyricists claim that the reason they love music so much is because it takes them away to another place. Stephen Sondheim is noted with saying, "If I cannot fly, let me sing." In Jesus' kingdom, singing is a pretty big deal. Throughout the ages, singing has been one of the primary ways that God's people have reminded themselves of God's salvation plan. Many of the psalms, known as songs of lament, demonstrate how God's people were still willing to sing even while they were caught in the middle of despair-filled circumstances, questioning God's faithfulness.

Singing in times of despair isn't uncommon; in fact, some historians have noted that Jesus may have been singing while dying on the cross.

In the first century, Jewish teachers (rabbis) had many creative styles of teaching. One of the teaching techniques that the rabbis utilized was called *remez*. *Remez* was kind of like a pop quiz. The rabbi would quote only the first line of a larger section of Scripture and his disciples were expected to recall the rest of the passage from memory.

Since Jesus was a first-century Jewish rabbi, it is likely that Jesus used *remez* with his disciples on a regular basis.

There is good reason to believe that Jesus was using *remez* from the cross when he quoted the first line of Psalm 22: "My God, my God, why have you forsaken me?" Jesus wasn't simply expressing his displeasure toward his heavenly Father; Jesus was giving his disciples a pop quiz at the foot of the cross.

Even in Jesus' last moments, when they were questioning everything, he was teaching his disciples how to trust in God's plan of salvation.

When the disciples heard Jesus quote psalm 22:1, their minds would have instantly jumped to the rest of the psalm. Psalm 22 was a very popular psalm in the first century, and it is very likely that Jesus' disciples knew how the psalm began and ended. Psalm 22 begins with multiple images of despair and agony, but in verse 19 the tone of the psalm shifts from despair to hope. The psalm ends with the triumphant proclamation: "Future generations will be told about the Lord. They will proclaim his righteousness, declaring to a people yet unborn: *He has done it!*" (vv. 30–31, emphasis added).

So, when Jesus asked, "My God my God why have you forsaken me?" he was actually trying to paint images of hope for his disciples. Jesus wanted his disciples to know that God was up to something good even in the midst of his present despair.

Furthermore, during the age of Jesus, psalms were considered the hymns or worship songs of the day. Each psalm could be sung and there were memorable rhythms which accompanied the lyrics. We know that Jesus sang hymns with his disciples. In fact, in Matthew 26:30, we see Jesus and his disciples singing a hymn just after their last supper and before they depart for the garden of Gethsemane.

It is unknown what psalm Jesus and his disciples had sung before they departed for the garden, but it is very possible that they were singing Psalm 22.

So, when Jesus sang the beginning of Psalm 22 from the cross, Jesus was basically reminding his disciples that *he* was the spectacular act that future generations were going to hear about. Jesus was claiming himself to be the hope of the world! Salvation is here!

As Jesus' disciples stood at the foot of the cross, we can imagine that they felt all kinds of fears, especially since it looked like all of their hope for salvation, their hope in Jesus, was questionable. I suspect we have all felt that way before. However, maybe the image of Jesus singing from the cross will help us overcome our fear of wondering if God's salvation is real.

Take a moment and reflect on Psalm 22 for yourself and imagine Jesus singing those words over you.

ideas to remember

God came to rescue us in this life and the life to come.

God's salvation doesn't start when we pass on; it starts right now.

Waiting on God leads to wanting more of God.

God longs to shine through us.

Don't mope; trust in God's hope.

questions to discuss

Do you struggle to accept salvation in the life to come? Why?

Do you struggle to accept salvation in this life? Why?

What difference does it make in your life to believe heaven starts on earth?

How would your life be different if you believed Jesus was living in your body and longing to shine through you?

What does living in the "hope of salvation" mean to you?

8

when you
feel like
a failure

If you're so fearful of failure that you never
set up your row of tin cans to shoot at, you're
not very likely to hit any at all. Failure is
not the end. For the person who determines
to learn from it, failure is a friend.

—Ralph F. Wilson

This is my command—be strong and courageous!
Do not be afraid or discouraged. For the Lord
your God is with you wherever you go.

—Joshua 1:9 nlt

I don't know anyone who likes to fail.

Failure makes us feel disappointed, angry, frustrated, sad, regretful, and confused.

People who have fears related to failure are motivated to avoid failing, not because they cannot manage the negative emotions attached to their fear, but because failure also makes them feel deep shame.

Shame is toxic because instead of feeling bad about our abilities or actions, it makes us feel bad about who we are. Shame corrodes the core of our being, making us incapable of interior change and external progress.

One psychologist has noted ten signs that indicate that you might fear failure. Check out these insights to see if you qualify:

1. Failing makes you worry about what other people think about you.

2. Failing makes you worry about your ability to pursue the future you desire.

3. Failing makes you worry that people will lose interest in you.

4. Failing makes you worry about how smart or capable you are.

5. Failing makes you worry about disappointing people whose opinion you value.

6. You tend to tell people beforehand that you don't expect to succeed in order to lower their expectations.

7. Once you fail at something you have trouble imagining what you could have done differently to succeed.

8. You often get last-minute headaches, stomachaches, or other physical symptoms that prevent you from completing your preparation.

9. You often get distracted by tasks that prevent you from completing your preparation that in hindsight were not as urgent as they seemed at the time.

10. You tend to procrastinate and run out of time to complete your preparation adequately.[1]

Does anyone not struggle with the fear of failure?

A few years ago, I reached a breaking point in my life and ministry. I was done. I knew something was deeply wrong with me, but I couldn't pinpoint what it was. I was high-strung, anxious, and couldn't sleep. Because of this, I was edgy, grumpy, and flat-out rude. I still remember the moment when my wife turned to me and said, "I want the old Ed back." This was my watershed moment and turning point.

I knew I needed deep change, so I set out to discover the root of my problems. I went through a three-week counseling experience, during which I learned a lot about myself. I was finally brought to the point where I could acknowledge my workaholic tendencies. My first reaction to this discovery was to try to work on it. Imagine that!

Through several counseling sessions, I discovered my workaholism wasn't fueled by a desire to succeed or be recognized, which is the case for some people. My workaholism was fueled by a deep fear of failure. For many reasons, tracing back to my childhood, I could not fail.

One of my counselor's suggestions for overcoming my fear of failure was to, well, fail. Genius, right? Even though it may have seemed like controlled failure, I took his advice and set up a series of events where I would experience the depths of my failure. I needed to arrive at the place where my identity was completely in Christ, not in my achievements. Let me tell you, failing was hard. But it was also worth it. I became a failure and was proud of it!

seeing new potential

In Matthew 28:1–10, we read a post-resurrection story where Mary and the disciples saw new potential in their lives and in Jesus' mission. They were encouraged to let go of their fear of failure and head into a Spirit-driven life. Here is the wonderful experience:

After the Sabbath, at dawn on the first day of the week, Mary Magdalene and the other Mary went to look at the tomb.

There was a violent earthquake, for an angel of the Lord came down from heaven and, going to the tomb, rolled back the stone and sat on it. His appearance was like lightning, and his clothes were white as snow. The guards were so afraid of him that they shook and became like dead men.

The angel said to the women, "[Fear not], for I know that you are looking for Jesus, who was crucified. He is not here; he has risen, just as he said. Come and see the place where he lay. Then go quickly and tell his disciples: 'He has risen from the dead and is going ahead of you into Galilee. There you will see him.' Now I have told you."

So the women hurried away from the tomb, afraid yet filled with joy, and ran to tell his disciples. Suddenly Jesus met them. "Greetings," he said. They came to him, clasped his feet and worshiped him. Then Jesus said to them, "[Fear not]. Go and tell my brothers to go to Galilee; there they will see me."

Jesus had died. It was an unmistakable death. Jesus had been beaten, whipped, hung on a cross, and had even experienced a spear through his heart.

Jesus literally died of a broken heart.

Like good Jews, the disciples moved quickly and set into motion the standard burial rituals. Jesus was wrapped in linens and placed in a tomb. On the third day, the women went to the tomb to finish their burial rituals, only to discover Jesus' body wasn't there.

Now, think about what was going on in Jesus' disciples' hearts and minds for a moment. For three years, Jesus had been preparing them for leadership within God's kingdom. Most of Jesus' disciples were still envisioning a movement where Jesus would push the oppressive Roman rulers out of power and allow the Jewish people to rule themselves and worship God freely. It makes sense that, after Jesus' death, the disciples were at a loss. What they thought was supposed to happen was not going to happen with a corpse.

It was over. Apparently, Jesus wasn't the messiah, and God's people would be required to wait even longer for their salvation to come. Just like the many other wannabe messiah movements, the mission Jesus initiated had failed. Furthermore, not only had the mission failed, but the disciples were also failures.

We can imagine the disciples were wondering things like, "What could we have done differently? What if we had stayed in the garden and fought the Roman guards? What if we had rescued Jesus?" Without a doubt, each one of the disciples felt like a failure—a failure to their families, a failure to themselves, and a failure to Jesus.

We can imagine, with heads hung low, the disciples were preparing to return to their family's line of work and try to blend back into society.

For the disciples, taking great risks for God was out of the question. Never again would they make that kind of sacrifice. Following another potential messiah around with the hope of the kingdom of God coming would not have sounded appealing. They were done.

That was, until the encounter at the tomb. When Jesus addressed the women, he began with those two life-changing words—*fear not*. Then Jesus immediately instructed the women to go and tell the other disciples he was alive and they would see him soon. This would have been a shocking message to hear.

On the first resurrection Sunday, when the women arrived at the tomb, they were certainly not prepared to receive the resurrection notification from God's messenger. Nor were they prepared to see Jesus alive. Can you imagine what that moment would have been like?

Jesus' resurrection changed everything. The women's painful sense of failure was turned into a beautiful sense of fulfillment. If Jesus wasn't dead, then the movement was alive. If the movement was alive, then they had a new purpose.

repurposed

I suspect most of us can relate to the disciples' debilitating fear of failure. I know I can.

In 2009 our first church plant was preparing to solidify our work in the community by buying property and building a facility which could serve as our ministry center. We had our hearts set on a beautiful piece of property on the west side of town near the interstate.

Prayers were being said, plans were being made, and people were behind the vision. We moved forward with the generosity campaign, hoping to raise the necessary funds for the project. It seemed like everything was coming together until midway through the campaign when we came across a significant roadblock. We discovered the land didn't perc, which meant the soil would not properly support a facility and we couldn't build on that particular site.

I was at a loss for what to do. Everything we were working toward and casting vision for halted. I felt like an idiot, a failure, and I knew my credibility was on the line. At some point, I was going to have to face the facts and break the news to our church.

My chats with God were not very nice. I was mad. Why would God lead me toward this vision only to set me up for failure?

One day, I was driving through town, praying for the Lord's help. Out of the corner of my eye, I happened to notice a new "For Sale" sign in a strip mall located right in the heart of town. I know it might sound crazy, but the Spirit convinced me this location was where our church was supposed to be.

I quickly contacted the realtor and explored the facility. It was perfect. I then walked the leaders of our church through the space, and everyone agreed, we were moving in the right direction.

The following week, I shared the news and presented the new plan. I feared complete rejection. However, what I received was complete receptivity. Everyone embraced the new vision, and within a few short months, we were gathering in our new facility.

It's interesting how God will take our greatest failures and turn them into our greatest accomplishments. Maybe our failures are God's way of reminding us of his faithfulness. Taking a great mess and turning it into greatness seems to be God's preferred way of operating.

For instance, Saul, who was an accomplice to the murder and persecution of many early Christians, ended up encountering the living Jesus and found himself a part of the group he formerly persecuted. The Lord changed Saul's name to Paul, gave him a new purpose, and called him to be one of the key influencers within the early church. It's interesting to read Paul's letters later in his life and hear him remind his churches that Christ Jesus came into the world to save sinners—of whom he was the worst (see 1 Tim. 1:15). For he knew firsthand how God can take an individual's great mess of a life and turn it into greatness.

Apparently, God likes to repurpose his people.

keep swingin'

Babe Ruth was once baseball's all-time home-run king. But did you know he was also the all-time strikeout champion? He struck out almost twice as often as he hit home runs. He knew he had to risk striking out in order to hit those home runs. When asked for the secret of his success, Ruth replied, "I just keep on swingin' at 'em!"[2]

Babe Ruth's story is inspiring because he didn't let his failures hinder him. He just kept on swingin'.

Recently, I was walking a young preacher through the aftershocks of preaching his first message. Any preacher can testify that the anxiety leading up to his or her first message is nothing compared to the anxiety afterward. I typically tell new preachers to reserve plenty of prayer time after their preaching, because that's when the Evil One likes to pounce. Many first-time preachers feel absolutely terrible after their first message and wonder if they should ever do it again. In those moments, I like to mention Babe Ruth's story and remind them to keep swingin'.

When we are tempted to give up after what may have seemed like a failure, it's good to remind ourselves of those times when God turned an individual around and they made an unforgettable comeback.

The story of the women seeing Jesus after he rose from the dead is one of those great comeback stories. We can envision the women running back to the other disciples, full of faith, shouting, "It's not over! It's not over!"

In our lives, we will fail at things. Maybe we'll fail at a business endeavor. Maybe we'll fail at a new church start. Maybe we'll fail in a friendship. Or maybe we'll fail in a ministry role. Whatever it will be, it is important to know that failure is not final.

Winston Churchill had it right when he said, "Success is never final; failure is never fatal; it is the courage to continue that counts."[3]

Try to identify the historical figure from the following account:

When I was seven years old, my family was forced out of our home because of a legal technicality. I had to work to help support my family. At age nine, while still a backward, shy little boy, my mother died. At age twenty-two, I lost my job as a store clerk. I wanted to go to law school but my education wasn't good enough. At twenty-three, I went into debt to become a partner in a small store. Three years later my partner died, leaving me a huge debt which took years to repay. At twenty-eight, after developing a romance with a young lady for four years, I asked her to marry me. She said no. At thirty-seven, on my third try, I was finally elected to the United States Congress. Two years later, I ran again and failed to be reelected. I had a nervous breakdown at that time. At forty-one, adding additional heartache to an already unhappy marriage, my four-year-old son died. The next year I ran for land officer and lost. At forty-five, I ran for the Senate and lost. A few years later, I ran for the vice presidency and lost. At forty-nine, I ran for the Senate again and lost. And at fifty-one, I was elected president of the United States. Who am I?

Does Abraham Lincoln ring a bell?

By all accounts, Lincoln's life was one continuous failure. But he kept on swingin' and became one of the greatest presidents in American history. He realized failure is not final.

I love the illuminating story of Thomas Edison. When Edison was attempting to invent the light bulb, he experienced over ten thousand failures before he discovered the right filament. Once Edison finally succeeded, he said, "I have not failed. I've just found [ten thousand] ways that won't work."[4]

Imagine what would happen to our fear of failure if we quit making excuses and looked at our lives through Edison's lens.

no mo' excuses

Do you remember the story of Moses and the burning bush? God called Moses to deliver his people and Moses rattled off all of his excuses as to why he was not the man for the job.

First Moses said, "Who am I? I'm a nobody?" God responded, "It doesn't matter who you are! I will be with you."

Next Moses said, "I'm not smart enough. I don't even know your name! What will I tell them?" God responded, "I am who I am." How do you argue with that?

Then Moses said, "I'm not talented enough. What if nobody listens to me?" God responded by changing Moses' staff into a snake, changing the appearance of Moses' hand, and changing water into blood.

We might think this would be enough, but Moses came up with yet another excuse. He declared, "I'm not qualified. I don't even talk well." God responded, "Your brother-in-law, Aaron, will help you" (see Ex. 3).

For every excuse, God shut down Moses.

It's foolish to argue with God, isn't it?

When we say, "Not me!" God says, "Remember, it's not about you—it's about me!"

Maybe you can relate to Moses. Maybe you're afraid to advance God's mission in this world because you're afraid of failure. Maybe you've laid out all of your excuses and have settled into the comforts of Mediocreville.

God would like to respond. I suspect you know what he's saying.

All too often we are like the African impala. The impala can jump to a height of over ten feet and cover a distance of greater than thirty feet in one leap. Yet these amazing creatures can be kept in an enclosure in any zoo with a three-foot wall. The animals will not jump if they can't see where their feet will land.[5]

As God's people, we don't know how everything is laid out. We don't know what the other side looks like. However, we must ask ourselves, is life in the zoo really better than life on the free range? Maybe it's time to muster up the courage and jump.

ideas to remember

The fear of failure is a precursor to great faith.

God can turn our great mess into greatness.

Failure is not final.

Faithful followers of Jesus keep swingin'.

There are no good excuses.

questions to discuss

Do you fear failure? Why?

Has your fear of failure ever stopped you from fulfilling your greatest potential?

Why do we struggle to view our potential failings as opportunities for great faith?

Have you given up on a God-given dream? If so, what fear is holding you back?

What excuses are you making to God?

9

when
life gets hard

The brick walls are there for a reason.
The brick walls are not there to keep us out.
The brick walls are there to give us a chance
to show how badly we want something.

—RANDY PAUSCH

I am leaving you with a gift—peace of mind and heart.
And the peace I give is a gift the world cannot give.
So don't be troubled or afraid.

—JOHN 14:27 NLT

Many years ago, before my busy family and professional life, a friend of mine challenged me to enter a half-marathon race with him. Since I didn't have anything better to do, I agreed to the challenge. My usual running routine was about four miles, so 12.6 miles seemed like quite a stretch. Yet I figured I was in good enough shape. Little did I know!

On the day of the race I knew my body was about to be tested to its core. The starting whistle blew, and I took off with an extra hop in my step. "I've got this; no worries," I thought to myself. I kept a pretty good pace alongside my running partner for about the first five miles, but then I slowly drifted behind.

Every stride became harder. Each mile marker seemed like forever. My graceful run quickly turned into an awkward-looking trot. To some, it might have been considered a quirky walk.

At mile eight, I thought I was about to die and meet my Lord. My legs were quivering and my head was spinning. I felt like I was about to pass out. However, I didn't want to stop, because I knew if I stopped, my muscles would lock up and I'd be finished. So I mustered up all of my energy and continued my awkward trot.

The last four miles became a blur. My legs felt like gelatin, and my mouth was as dry as the heart of a haystack. I really don't know how I made it to the finish line, but I did!

After the race, my running partner eventually found me lying on the ground, and in our pain, we celebrated our accomplishment together. I was quick to let my buddy know I was never going to do that again!

To this day, I'm proud to say, I have stayed faithful to my vow.

Life presents us with many challenges. I think it's safe to say we are challenged on a daily basis. We might be challenged by a workout program, a parenting task, or a ministry in our church.

It is important to realize a challenge can be viewed from two different angles. Challenges can either be problems or opportunities. How we view a challenge says more about us than about the challenge itself. The way we choose to see our challenges is the way our world will be.

accepting life's challenges

In Acts 27:21–26, we read of a time when the apostle Paul's life got hard and he was faced with a great challenge. Here is Paul's story:

> After they had gone a long time without food, Paul stood up before them and said: "Men, you should have taken my advice not to sail from Crete; then you would have spared yourselves this damage and loss. But now I urge you to keep up your courage, because not one of you will be lost; only the ship will be destroyed. Last night an angel of the God to whom I belong and whom I serve stood beside me and said, '[Fear not], Paul. You must stand trial before Caesar; and God has graciously given you the lives of all who sail with you.' So keep up your courage, men, for I have faith in God that it will happen just as he told me. Nevertheless, we must run aground on some island."

Paul was a diehard—a man of great courage. Remember, it was Paul, formerly known as Saul, who persecuted Christians in an attempt to wipe out the Jesus movement. After he encountered Jesus on the road to Damascus, Saul's name was changed to Paul, which symbolized his inner transformation. Paul's old life was gone, and his new life had begun.

In Paul's new life, he was on to the cause of Christ. We know enough about Paul to know he faced challenge after challenge and constantly risked his life so the message of Jesus could spread throughout the world.

In this particular missionary journey, Paul faced a double challenge. Paul's ship was in danger of being destroyed by the mighty sea. If Paul survived the shipwreck, then he would be required to face a trial before the all-powerful Caesar. Talk about one challenge after another!

In the midst of Paul's challenge, he rose to the occasion and took control of the situation. The prisoner became the courageous captain.

Paul boldly announced that a messenger of God had come to him and revealed how they would be protected from the storm. Notice the messenger began his statement with those two life-changing words— *fear not*. Then the messenger explained why Paul needed to survive the storm and that he must be at his trial before Caesar, because it would be an opportunity to spread the good news about Jesus.

Paul would have been living with the tension of the immediate danger of the sea. However, he also was living with the tension of knowing what Caesar could do with him once he was in his sights. Paul could have looked at the storm as a way to escape, but he didn't. He trusted the messenger's words and proceeded with great faith.

Paul wasn't looking at his challenges as set*backs*; he was looking at them as set*ups*!

growing from problems

When Emily and I were first married, we quickly discovered how different we really were. She washes her clothes; I "wersh" my clothes. She loves to go on walks and talks; I like sitting and silence. She is emotionally driven; I am logically driven. Even though we deeply love each other, everything about us is polar opposite.

Over the years, we have experienced the raw rub of our opposing viewpoints. Like every married couple, we have our conflicts and problems. Around our fifth year of marriage, we went to a marriage conference and came to realize that our problems weren't really problems. They were simply God's way of growing us deeper.

Friedrich Nietzsche once said, "That which does not kill us makes us stronger."[1] I would amend, "That which does not kill us makes us grow deeper."

Times of great difficulty are times of great opportunity to grow deeper in God's ways. Life's difficulties never feel ideal, but they usually provide keen insight into ideas of great value. For example, the entire book of Proverbs, a collection of God-inspired wise sayings, came from a man who had experienced some of life's greatest difficulties. Yet he presents us with many of the best solutions to life's challenges.

When times are good and everything is comfortable, it's easy to become complacent and forget how resourceful we are capable of being. It's in times of trouble when we discover incredible skills, allowing us to move beyond our fears.

Without a doubt, it's always easier to run from our problems. However, running from our problems may cause us to fall short of fulfilling our greatest potential in life. Even more significantly, running from our problems may not be God's will for our lives.

staying true to yourself

We blast into the world as babies, bursting with confidence and totally free to be ourselves. Every object is worthy to explore and stick in our mouths. Life seems like one big adventure after another.

We are born into a world full of prospects and with the potential to achieve incredible things, but somewhere along the way, as we enter into adulthood, our audacious childhood drive begins to wither away.

From the very day we are born, we are subjected to social conditioning from our parents, teachers, friends, and the media. We're taught how to fit in and form to the expected mold.

It's no surprise, then, that gradually over the years, many of us begin to lose our sense of identity, struggle to understand who we really are, and feel incredibly misplaced in life.

Sadly, we often hide our dreams and compromise our core values in order to be accepted by others. By the time we reach adulthood, we have created a whole belief system based on what we've been told as we've grown up.

As I was growing up, our family adopted a spunky black lab puppy. When he came into our family, he had already been given the name Key. We eventually changed his name to Luckey in order to make him feel like he was ours. However, we quickly discovered why our pup was originally named Key. Apparently, Key was so good at escaping whatever enclosure he was placed in, it was like he had a key to the kennel. When our family had Luckey, he would escape by climbing the six-foot fence, digging holes underneath the fence, or undoing the kennel latch.

Even though we changed Luckey's name by a hair, Luckey knew who he was. Luckey was a purebred escape artist, and he wasn't about to compromise his original identity just because his surroundings had changed.

When challenges arise, we will be tempted to compromise our core values, morals, and commitments to God. We'll be tempted to be someone else. We will discover it's easier to compromise in these core areas than face the sticky situations we might find ourselves in.

In Paul's life, there were many points were he could have taken an easier route. Paul could have chosen to live a trouble-free life. Before Paul encountered Jesus, he was already a well-respected Jewish Pharisee. He was set socially, relationally, and financially. But God wanted him to set others up with the way, the truth, and the life. At any point, Paul could have gone back to a life of ease, but he didn't. Paul chose to stay the course and fulfill God's purposes.

We too have a choice to stay on God's path or venture off on our own. Staying on God's path means we will stay true to ourselves as we watch our dreams come alive.

pursuing your dreams

When my wife and I go on long road trips, we always ask each other in goofy voices: "What are your hopes and dreams?" This question seems to stir our hearts and reunite our original vision for our union. It has been neat to see some of our dreams become reality. Looking back, one thing is for certain—our dreams didn't just happen. We had to work hard and fight for our dreams to come true.

Many times, when something goes wrong or a dream seems difficult, we assume it wasn't meant to be. Dreams do not happen overnight, but they do happen if we continue to pursue them. When things don't go right, it doesn't mean we ought to lose hope.

Goals and dreams are kind of like breathing. We breathe in and out anywhere from fifteen to twenty-five times per minute without even thinking about it. We can't stop ourselves from breathing even if we try. Even when we exercise, we don't have to think about breathing. Breathing is a natural bodily function. In the same way, our God-given dreams should flow just as naturally. If we give up on our dreams, we give up on life to the fullest.

To be sure, there's always going to be something trying to suffocate our dreams. Sometimes it's an outside influence. Sometimes it's a deep inner fear. It is important to know the difference.

being present

When we fear life's difficulties, we may be tempted to try to live in the past or the future. However, we need to understand we were made to exist in the here and now.

Have you ever been around someone who is living in the pristine past? Or have you ever been around someone who is living in a future façade?

Time is a very misleading thing. All there ever is, is the now. We can gain experience from the past, and we can hope for the future. However, we can't relive our past, and we don't really know the shape of our future. We can ruin today by focusing on another time and place.

Being present matters most.

Presentness is one of the most convicting topics. In today's consumer-driven culture, we all find ourselves distracted by the diversions life throws at us on a daily basis.

If anybody was an advocate for present-living, it was Jesus. One time Jesus used a parable about seeds and a sower to expound on his desire for his disciples to live in the present realm with him. Here is Jesus' explanation of his parable:

> Listen then to what the parable of the sower means: When anyone hears the message about the kingdom and does not understand it, the evil one comes and snatches away what was sown in their heart. This is the seed sown along the path. The seed falling on rocky ground refers to someone who hears the word and at once receives it with joy. But since they have no root, they last only a short time. When trouble or persecution comes because of the word, they quickly fall away. The seed falling among the thorns refers to someone who hears the word, but the worries of this life and the deceitfulness of wealth choke the word, making it unfruitful. But the seed falling on good soil refers to someone who hears the word and understands it. This is the one who produces a crop, yielding a hundred, sixty or thirty times what was sown. (Matt. 13:18–23)

Isn't it interesting that each seed or person who isn't planted in the good soil is attempting to live in a moment other than the present? Those who live with a remember-when or one-day mentality will struggle to conquer the fears connected to life's hardships. However, those who are firmly rooted in the good soil of God will be fruitful and fulfilled.

Few people in Jesus' day, or even today, fully understand Jesus' plea to be present with him at all times. Jesus' parable would have caused some of his hearers to question where they were planted.

"What kind of soil am I planted in?" is a very important question.

If we know we have been planted in the good soil, maybe we just need to let our roots grow deep and become more aware of the power within the present moment.

being thankful

As we live in the here and now, we can't help but begin to develop a grateful heart. Present-living presents us with a gift—the ability to endure any hardship or difficulty with a hope-filled attitude.

In 1 Thessalonians 5:16–18, Paul said, "Rejoice *always*, pray continually, give thanks in *all* circumstances; for this is God's will for you in Christ Jesus" (emphasis added).

King David said, I will praise the LORD at *all* times. I will *constantly* speak his praises" (Ps. 34:1 NLT, emphasis added).

When reading these Scriptures, we may wonder how it is possible to be thankful all the time. In the midst of painful situations, we may feel like our lives have been shattered into a million pieces. It is important to know God isn't instructing us to be thankful *for* difficult circumstances; God is instructing us to be thankful *in* the difficult circumstances. When we are thankful in difficult times, our attitude says to God, "I trust you. I know we'll get through this and you will be glorified when it's all said and done."

Recently, a good friend of mine was vacationing in Florida with his wife. After a fun day at the beach, they returned to their room, planning on enjoying a relaxing evening together. Everything seemed good, until my friend found his wife lying on the floor in an unconscious state. He quickly called 9-1-1 and held his wife until the ambulance came. The paramedics rushed her to the hospital. Later in the evening, he learned she had a life-shattering stroke.

For several months, my friend was caught in the middle of a terrible circumstance. Not only did he have to take care of his wife, but he also had to fly back to Michigan to manage his work life as she recovered. On one occasion, he was able to attend our church's worship gathering, and he shared how God was comforting him in his time of need. After the gathering, he flew back to Florida and posted these profound words on Facebook:

A little more than a month ago I walked the beaches of Florida with my wife. Now I walk them alone. I don't write this to make anyone feel sorry for me, but as a caution. Even after a few years of marriage, many people feel like throwing in the towel for various reasons. It may even seem easier to move on rather than live with discontentment or pain. However, when you have stood at the bedside of your spouse for months, like I have, not knowing what they are going through and to what extent your life has irrevocably changed, you will fall to your knees and beg God for them back.

Please take my advice. Take an evening and look around the house and notice the tiniest things they do for you. Look at their clothes and their favorite possessions. Then, imagine life with them in the hospital fighting for their lives. Anger and hurt can drive you to want to cash it all in, but when you experience loss this way, you find out how much you really love them. Appreciate your spouse and family tonight when you go home and thank God for them.

In the midst of great pain, my friend was able to remain thankful because he knew God would not fail him. Month after month, he relied upon God, and God saw him through his troubles.

Life is full of twists and turns, and sometimes we fall upon hard times. No matter what the circumstances, we can rest in the fact that God is faithful. God will hold us in the hollow of his hand, and he will help us through our hardship.

When life gets hard, we will eventually be tempted to cramp up in fear. However, if we keep our face toward the Son, the shadows will fall behind.

ideas to remember

Challenges can be viewed as problems or opportunities.

Never compromise core values.

Hardships will grow us deeper in God's ways.

No matter how hard it gets, don't stop pursuing God-given dreams.

Live in the here and now.

Rejoice in sufferings.

questions to discuss

Why do you tend to run from your problems instead of embracing them?

Do you view life's challenges as problems or opportunities?

In the midst of a challenge, have you ever felt tempted to compromise your core values and commitment to God?

How has a challenge grown you deeper in God's ways?

What God-given dream have you let slip away?

Why is it so hard to live in the present?

10

when you
doubt
God's presence

I will not fear, for You are ever with me,
and You will never leave me
to face my perils alone.

—Thomas Merton

And I am convinced that nothing can ever separate
us from God's love. Neither death nor life, neither angels
nor demons, neither our fears for today nor our worries
about tomorrow—not even the powers of hell
can separate us from God's love.

—Romans 8:38 NLT

One of the most frustrating things in the world is to be ignored.

Recently, all three of my children snuck downstairs to watch TV after their mother had told them not to. Emily knew what they were up to, and she gave me the look that said, "Are you going to do anything about this?" I took my cue and called for them to come upstairs, but not one of them answered me. I called a second time. No one answered. The irritation was building. I called a third time, with an edge of seriousness to my voice. No one answered. This was not good.

With a heavy foot, I started downstairs. I happened to notice a little scurrying around the corner. So I called again. No one answered. Finally, my irritation meter was about maxed out, and I raised my voice: "Answer me when I call for you!"

Sometimes we approach God the way I was approaching my children. Often, it seems like God is ignoring us. When we call out for God to respond, our voice is met with silence. We may wonder, is God hiding? Is God no longer present? Why won't God respond?

Since we can't usually see God or audibly hear him, it's easy to doubt his presence. Many times, if it seems God has not been present for a while, we may even fear God is no longer near.

the nearness of God

After Jesus' death and resurrection, many of Jesus' disciples had genuine doubts about God's presence in the world. When Jesus was with his disciples on earth, they could ask Jesus questions, share their heart with him, or crack a joke, and he would immediately respond. However, after Jesus rejoined his Father in the heavenly realm, everything was different.

We can imagine the disciples longed for Jesus' physical presence. Yet, like us, they were required to utilize a sixth sense and discover God's presence through his guiding Spirit and times of prayer.

One of the early disciples called upon to build up the church of Jesus Christ was named John. This particular John penned the book of Revelation—a circulatory letter written to seven specific churches in Asia Minor, with the purpose of revealing and reminding the churches who Jesus was, is, and is to come.

This revelation of Jesus Christ was timely. Throughout the first century, the early church was experiencing immense persecution from the Roman authorities. It wasn't easy to be a Christian. Church tradition informs us that the majority of Jesus' original disciples were martyred for the faith. During this era, many of the early followers of Jesus were losing hope and wondering if the way of Jesus was still worth it. Revelation was written to bring Jesus-followers hope and to clarify the church's purpose in the world.

John tipped us off to his environment early in his book. He noted he was writing from the island of Patmos. From historical records, we know Patmos was not the type of island people went to in order to escape the routines of life and bask in the sun. Not even close. Patmos was an island of exile, where the Roman authorities banished people who were considered a threat to the Roman Empire.[1] Knowing John was uprooted from his normal life and forced to live out his days on an island with other prisoners helps us understand the overarching intent of Revelation.

We can imagine John had many moments when he felt entirely abandoned by God and feared his absence. In John's former role, he was an overseer of several churches and would have had many encouraging people around him. Yet on Patmos, he didn't have anyone. He was alone. However, it was on this island and in this context that John experienced the deepest level of God's presence.

Sometimes God does his deepest work in us when we feel the most abandoned.

In Revelation 1:17–20, John shared his vision of Jesus with his church network and reminded them of God's everlasting presence. Here is a glimpse into John's vision of Jesus:

> When I saw him, I fell at his feet as though dead. Then he placed his right hand on me and said: "[Fear not]. I am the First and the Last. I am the Living One; I was dead, and now look, I am alive forever and ever! And I hold the keys of death and Hades. Write, therefore, what you have seen, what is now and what will take place later. The mystery of the seven stars that you saw in my right hand and of the seven golden lampstands is this: The seven stars are the angels of the seven churches, and the seven lampstands are the seven churches."

Notice, when Jesus saw John, the first words were those two life-changing words—*fear not*. Before Jesus could fully reveal himself to John, he needed John to release his fears, doubts, and feelings of abandonment.

Then Jesus described himself as the first and the last, which is a clear statement about his divinity. Jesus was not only there in the beginning of the world—he *was* the beginning. Likewise, Jesus will not only be there in the end—he *is* the end. As Colossians 1:17 declares, "He is before all things, and in him all things hold together."

Sometimes, when we feel like Jesus is no longer present, we need to remind ourselves that all of human history leads from and to Jesus. We live in his-story, whether we like it or not.

As John continued to write out his vision of Jesus for the church, both present and future, he tried to encourage followers of Jesus to continue advancing God's mission on earth, even when they felt isolated, alone, and abandoned. Everything, including their present suffering, would be worth it.

you are not alone

Throughout my life, I have experienced many bouts of loneliness. I remember the deep lonesomeness that came as a result of accepting my first ministry assignment as a twenty-year-old youth pastor. Following through with that particular assignment required me to move from Missouri to Michigan. Besides the church leaders who initially interviewed me, I didn't know anyone from Michigan. I packed up everything I owned in my 1971 Chevelle and started out on the journey to Michigan. One might assume I felt close to God, but truth be told, I never felt so distant. It wasn't a good feeling, but I knew I was headed in the right direction.

Surprisingly, even Mother Teresa, the remarkably faithful nun who served the poor and unwanted of Calcutta all her life, felt as if God had abandoned her for many years. References to internal darkness and feelings of being unloved by God fill her letters to her spiritual directors over the years.

One time, Mother Teresa wrote in her spiritual diary, "In my soul, I feel just the terrible pain of loss, of God not wanting me, of

141

God not being God, of God not really existing." In another letter she noted how she wanted to love God "like he has not been loved," and yet she felt her love was not reciprocated.

In the context of Mother Teresa's life, these types of thoughts are not heresy, but signs of holiness. Those closest to Mother Teresa have noted, despite her feelings, she was convinced God existed and had a plan for her life, even if she did not feel his presence. As she hurt on the inside, she maintained a lovely smile, kept working, and continued to rejoice in her mission.

In a 1961 letter to the Missionaries of Charity, she wrote, "Without suffering our work would just be social work. All the desolation of poor people must be redeemed and we must share in it."[2]

Mother Teresa knew how to remain fearless even when she doubted God's presence.

While some people may be surprised or even shocked by Mother Teresa's spiritual struggles, hopefully they serve as an inspiration for generations to come. Because the feeling of God being far away or even nonexistent is a common spiritual experience.

Loneliness may best be defined as longing for intimacy. We may not enjoy the feelings of distance from God, but we can still take what God gives us with a smile and stay faithful in the smallest things.

In the Christian tradition, we have a certain understanding of loneliness being an inevitable part of the human condition. We were created for complete union with God, but are unable to fully experience completeness this side of eternity. The important thing is to continue to express our feelings to God.

pour out your heart

Psalm 62:8 says, "Trust in him at all times, you people; pour out your hearts to him, for God is our refuge."

I'm terrible at expressing my emotions. I can go a long time without people realizing something is wrong with me on the inside. I tend to be a bit of a stuffer.

Since it is not natural for me to express my emotions, I have had to become disciplined in pouring out my heart. Over the years, I have noticed a connection between my ability to pour out my heart to God and my ability to pour out my heart to others. I suppose pouring out my heart to God is good practice for pouring out my heart to others.

In 1 Samuel 1, we glimpse a woman named Hannah, who is found in the temple of God, pouring out her heart before the Lord. Hannah's prayer is far more than just a prayer. Hannah is presenting her emotions before God in the most genuine manner.

For years, Hannah struggled with her barrenness. After a series of negative pokes from people around her, she made a vow in the temple and said, "LORD Almighty, if you will only look on your servant's misery and remember me, and not forget your servant but give her a son, then I will give him to the LORD for all the days of his life" (v. 11).

As she continued her prayer to the Lord, Eli, the priest observed her mouth. Hannah was praying in her heart. Her lips were moving, but her voice was not heard. Eli thought she was drunk. In 1 Samuel 1:15–16, Hannah replied, "I am a woman who is deeply troubled. I have not been drinking wine or beer; I was pouring out my soul to the LORD. Do not take your servant for a wicked woman; I have been praying here out of my great anguish and grief."

Hannah poured out her heart to God, because she knew God listens, cares, and had a plan for her life.

the one constant

Deuteronomy 31:6 says, "Be strong and courageous. Do not be afraid or terrified because of them, for the LORD your God goes *with* you; he will never leave you nor forsake you" (emphasis added).

God has promised us his constant presence.

Often, life experience will cause us to struggle with the words *never* and *always*. When we hear the words *never* and *always*, we instantly think of situations where *never* wasn't really never and *always* wasn't really always. Apparently, there are exceptions.

People may fail us. Even our best of friends may turn their backs on us. However, when it comes to God, he offers his constant presence to us, with no exceptions.

The question isn't, "Is God present?" The question is, "Am I present to God?" When we are conscious of God's presence every day, we experience a peace and joy which surpasses all understanding. As we abide in God's presence, we will find we begin to speak and behave like him. This is because we cannot be in God's presence without his beauty, love, peace, power, and glory rubbing off on us.

In the biblical narrative, there is far more emphasis on whom we worship than on how we worship. This is because our faith ancestors knew we will become like the one we worship. The values and characteristics of our God will seep into our lives and eventually overflow from our lives.

Jesus also believed in this principle. In John 8:12, Jesus told his disciples, "I am the light of the world. Whoever follows me will never walk in darkness, but will have the light of life." Then, in another teaching found in Matthew 5:14, Jesus turned to his disciples and said, "You are the light of the world. A town built on a hill cannot be hidden." Jesus knew, as his followers began living in him, the Light of the World, they would then have the experience of him lighting them up.

The great paradox of the Christian life is recognizing that the one thing our soul craves most, God's presence, can be found within us, as Christ's Spirit indwells us.

receiving Christ's strength

It was about 8:30 p.m. on a warm summer evening in Tucson, Arizona. Tom Boyle was sitting in the passenger's seat of his pickup truck, his wife Elizabeth at the wheel, waiting to pull out into traffic from the shopping mall where they'd just had dinner. The Camaro ahead of them hit the gas, spun his wheels, and jerked out onto the avenue with a squeal of rubber.

Boyle glanced up to see a shower of red sparks flying up from beneath the chassis of the Camaro. And something else—a bike, folded up from impact. The Camaro had hit a cyclist, and the rider was pinned underneath the car. Boyle threw open the door of the truck and ran after the car.

For a few gruesome seconds, the Camaro plunged on and dragged along the rider, eighteen-year-old Kyle Holtrust, with it. One of Holtrust's legs was pinned between the chassis of the car and the frame of his bike, the other was jammed between the bike and the asphalt. After twenty or thirty feet, the Camaro slowed and stopped. Holtrust screamed in agony as he pounded on the side of the car with his free hand.

Without stopping to think, Boyle reached under the frame of the car and lifted. With a sound of groaning metal, the chassis eased upward a few inches. "Mister, mister, higher, higher," Holtrust screamed.

Boyle braced himself, took a deep breath, and heaved. The front end lifted a few more inches. "OK, it's off me," the boy called out, his voice tight with pain. "But I can't move. Get me out!" The driver of the car, forty-year-old John Baggett, pulled Holtrust free. At last, about forty-five seconds after he'd first heaved the car upward, Boyle set it back down.

The biker was badly hurt, in a lot of pain, and frightened. Blood poured out of his wounds. Boyle knelt and wrapped the young man in his arms, comforting him until the police and fire departments arrived.

The local media celebrated Boyle's feat of compassion. The YMCA gave him an award. Newspapers and TV stations interviewed him. The fanfare flattered him, and he felt extremely proud of himself. Yet to this day there's something about that evening he can't figure out. It's no mystery to him why he did what he did, but he can't quite figure out how. Something extraordinary was going on.[3]

That something was the body's response to fear. When we find ourselves under intense pressure, fear unleashes reserves of energy that normally remain inaccessible. We become, in effect, superhuman.

Under acute stress, the body's sympathetic nervous system prepares the body for sustained, vigorous action. The adrenal gland dumps cortisol and adrenaline into the blood stream. Blood pressure surges and the heart races, delivering oxygen and energy to the muscles. It's the biological equivalent of opening the throttle of an engine.

Similar to the way Boyle received a seemingly supernatural strength in a moment of fear, we too can receive Christ's strength in our moments of fear. We may live most of our life doubting God's presence, but all it takes is one moment where we experience a deep inner strength beyond our normal capacities, and we will be convinced God's presence is real.

These are the moments which make up our irrevocable story.

remember well

It's interesting how often the Scriptures utilize the word *remember*. Remembering is the process of bringing our memories back together.

Shortly after God delivered his people from Egyptian slavery, he began to prepare his people for the Promised Land, the land flowing with cows and bees. In Deuteronomy 6:12, God said, "Be careful that you do not forget the LORD, who brought you out of Egypt, out of the land of slavery." It's baffling to think God's people needed to be reminded of their delivery. Yet God knew his creation had a tendency to forget. So God reminded them to remember how he came through for them in their time of need.

One of the first songs recorded in Scripture comes shortly after the great exodus out of Egypt. In Exodus 15:1–2, Moses and the Israelites sang this song to the Lord: "I will sing to the LORD, for he is highly exalted. Both horse and driver he has hurled into the sea.

The LORD is my strength and my defense; he has become my salvation. He is my God, and I will praise him, my father's God, and I will exalt him." For God's people, singing spiritual songs became a way of remembering God's presence in their lives.

To be sure, great exodus-like stories don't happen to us every day, but we'd do well to keep those moments at the forefront of our hearts and minds and pass them on from generation to generation.

In Deuteronomy 6:4–9, Moses drove home this transgenerational principle by declaring, "Hear, O Israel: The LORD our God, the LORD is one. Love the LORD your God with all your heart and with all your soul and with all your strength. These commandments that I give you today are to be on your hearts. Impress them on your children. Talk about them when you sit at home and when you walk along the road, when you lie down and when you get up. Tie them as symbols on your hands and bind them on your foreheads. Write them on the doorframes of your houses and on your gates." In other words, don't ever, ever forget!

Let's face it. We need more reminders of God's presence in our lives. Sometimes we suffer from faith amnesia. It doesn't take much to look back on our lives and notice what God has done for us and what he has brought us through.

If you recall, before Jesus took up his cross, he told his disciples to take some bread and wine every time they had dinner together in the future, and remember his broken body and his blood which would be shed. Jesus was setting up a new tradition for his faithful followers to remember what he did for them. To remember how their sins were forgiven. To remember how they were given strength to overcome the world. And to remember to *fear not*—for he would always be with them.

What are we to do when we are overwhelmed? What are we to do when we have no strength and nowhere to turn? What are we to do when we are not able to do much about the obstacles in our path? What are we to do when we are weak and powerless to change anything? What are we to do when we are on a collision course with the future? What are we to do when forces are tearing away at us and undermining all we try to do?

Come to Jesus.

He has helped us before and he will help us again. He has been our supplier of strength and power when we had no strength and power of our own. He has never failed us. He has given us more than we could ever dream of seeking. He has enabled us to do what we thought was impossible to do. He has enabled us to move mountains.

Praise the name of Jesus.

ideas to remember

Sometimes God does his deepest work in us when we feel the most abandoned.

All of human history leads from and to Jesus.

Remain fearless even when you doubt God's presence.

God's constant presence can always be experienced.

Remember.

questions to discuss

When was a time you felt abandoned by God?

Why do we doubt God's presence in our lives?

Why does God use our experiences of abandonment to do a deeper work in us?

Why do we tend to forget the way in which God has worked in and through our life?

If you were to share your faith with your children, what stories would emerge where God's presence became real to you?

afterword

your next shot

Some say if only my fears and doubts will leave then I will get to work. But instead you should get to work and then your fears and doubts will leave.

—Dwight L. Moody

Even though I walk through the darkest valley, I will fear no evil, for you are with me.

—Psalm 23:4

With a tied score and four seconds left on the clock, I found myself on the foul line, and the game-winning shot was in the palm of my hand. My heart pounded. My nerves twitched. My entire school watched.

I knew if I made at least one of the two shots, I would go down in my school's history as a hero. But, if I missed both of the shots, I would be ridiculed for the rest of my high school days. Everything in me wanted to run into the locker room and hide.

As I approached the free-throw line, my teammates surrounded me and reassured me of my shooting abilities. "Ed, you've got this. You can do it!" they exclaimed. Just before the referee passed me the ball, I took a deep breath and tried to release the tension I felt inside. Upon the exhale, the ball bounced into my hands. This was my moment. I dribbled my typical three times, lined up the seams, spun the ball backward, and let the ball fly.

Clank!

The crowd gasped.

"No worries, Ed; you've got this one," screamed my coach from the sidelines.

Now panic set in. My heart was somewhere near my throat. The roar of the crowd sounded like a freight train, but I tried to block it out as I made my way back to the line for my second opportunity to clinch the game.

Just as the referee was about to toss me the ball, the opposing team decided to call their final timeout. In basketball, this action is referred to as icing the shooter.

My teammates quickly dashed off to the sidelines and continued encouraging me along the way. Needless to say, the pressure was climaxing. Yet I kept telling myself, "You've got this, Ed.

You've made this shot a thousand times. This is your time to rise up!"

The timeout seemed to take forever. In due course, the buzzer sounded, and I confidently strutted up to the line. As the referee passed me the ball, he made it known, "One shot boys, one shot."

I dribbled three times, lined up the seams, spun the ball backward, and released.

Clank!

My greatest fear came true. I missed the shot! My teammates shook their heads. My coach looked down in frustration. My heart sunk. Not only had I been iced—I was crushed.

Sadly, our team went on to lose in overtime. All I wanted to do was crawl in a hole and never show my face again around school. After the game, my teammates didn't say anything to me, but they didn't have to—their silence said it all. I quickly scuffled out of the locker room, drove home, and beat myself up as I replayed the situation over and over in my mind.

One might think, after such an embarrassing moment, I would spend the better part of practice on the free-throw line, taking shot after shot in an attempt to redeem myself. But for some reason, I could not go near the line. It was as if there was a force field, or a fear field, that kept me away from the free-throw line.

Day after day, I avoided the dreadful fifteen-foot shot at all costs. It seemed easier to steer clear of the free-throw line than to face it head on. Yet I knew there would be a day when I would be fouled, and I would be required to shoot the shot that is anything but free.

Given that I certainly didn't want a repeat of the previous game, I decided to get it over with and face my fear. I was ready to plow through my fear field. With great buoyancy in my stride, I stepped

153

up to the line and prepared to shoot. I dribbled my typical three times, lined up the seams, spun the ball backward, and let the ball fly.

Swish! The ball went in!

It felt good to make a bucket, so I continued shooting. Each time the ball dropped through the net, my confidence rose. By some means, my greatest fear was becoming my greatest passion. With a newfound trust in my shot, I decided that day to make the free-throw shot *my* shot.

After I missed the game-winning points, I may have let my fears get the better of me for a period of time, but I didn't let my fears get the best of me. In a strange twist of irony, I went on to finish the season with the best free-throw record in our region.

In the game of life, there's always a next shot. We just have to be willing to take the first step.

Several years ago, I realized one of the primary tools of the Evil One was to ice us in fear. Because of my inner fears, I was missing out on fulfilling my greatest potential in life. I have climbed the mountain of fear long enough to know that the feeling of overcoming fear is much more satisfying than wallowing in the base-camp of ineffectiveness.

We will always struggle to conquer our deepest fears, but over time, we'll notice it gets easier the more we do it. When I think about how I have overcome many of my deepest fears, I can't say the answer was found in taking baby steps. Every time, the answer has seemed to be one giant step of faith.

The more I replace my fear with faith, the more I grow in my walk with God. After more than a decade of taking giant steps of faith, I can honestly say, it was always worth it. Not only have I been inspired to grow closer to God; I have watched others be inspired as well.

Nothing in this life is more satisfying than knowing a deep fear has been overcome and a deeper level of trust in God has been attained.

We regularly need to be reminded of those two life-changing words—*fear not*. Those two words are peppered throughout the biblical narrative for a reason. God desperately wants his followers to listen and obey his promptings.

So, what would it look like if you broke free of your greatest fears and allowed God to use you for his great purposes in the world?

Fear not, my friend.

notes

chapter 1
1. William Barclay, *The Gospel of Luke*, rev. ed., The Daily Study Bible Series (Louisville, KY: Westminster, 1975), 10.

chapter 3
1. William Barclay, *The Gospel of Luke*, rev. ed., The Daily Study Bible Series (Louisville, KY: Westminster, 1975), 22–23.

2. Dr. Payson, quoted in "Heart's Ease," sermon, August 27, 1865, by C. H. Spurgeon at the Metropolitan Tabernacle, accessed July 30, 2014, http://www.christalone.com/spurgeon-sermons/137-volume-11/2277-heart-s-ease.

chapter 4
1. William Barclay, *The Gospel of Luke*, rev. ed., The Daily Study Bible Series (Louisville, KY: Westminster, 1975), 57.

chapter 5
1. Charles Swindoll, *The Tale of the Tardy Oxcart: And 1,501 Other Stories* (Nashville: Thomas Nelson, 1998), 215–216.

2. Brennan Manning, *Lion and Lamb: The Relentless Tenderness of Jesus* (Grand Rapids, MI: Revell, 1986), 64.

chapter 6

1. Frank E. Graeff, "Does Jesus Care?" 1901, public domain, accessed July 30, 2014, http://library.timelesstruths.org/music/Does_Jesus_Care/.

2. William Barclay, *The Gospel of Luke*, rev. ed., The Daily Study Bible Series (Louisville, KY: Westminster, 1975), 101.

3. C. S. Lewis, *God in the Dock* (Grand Rapids, MI: Eerdmans, 1970), 75.

chapter 7

1. John Johnson, "Firefighter's 3 Kids Rescued, by His Own Wife," Newser.com, February 20, 2014, http://www.newser.com/story/182667/fire fighters-3-kids-rescued-by-his-own-wife.html.

2. William Barclay, *The Gospel of John*, rev. ed., The Daily Study Bible Series (Louisville, KY: Westminster, 1975), 115.

chapter 8

1. Guy Winch, "Ten Signs You Might Have a Fear of Failure," *The Squeaky Wheel* (blog), *Psychology Today*, June 18, 2013, http://www.psychology today.com/blog/the-squeaky-wheel/201306/ten-signs-you-might-have-fear-failure.

2. Robert J. Morgan, ed., *Nelson's Annual Preacher's Sourcebook*, 2004 ed. (Nashville: Thomas Nelson, 2004), 385.

3. "Thoughts On the Business of Life," *Forbes*, November 1948, 34.

4. As quoted in an ad for GPU Nuclear Corporation, *Black Enterprise* 16, no. 11 (June 1986): 79.

5. Craig Larson, *Illustrations for Preaching and Teaching* (Grand Rapids, MI: Baker, 1994), 78.

chapter 9

1. Friedrich Nietzsche, *Twilight of the Idols* (Oxford: Oxford University Press, 1888), 8.

chapter 10

1. Robert Mulholland, *Revelation: Holy Living in an Unholy World* (Grand Rapids, MI: Francis Asbury Press, 1980), 76–77.

2. Cindy Wooden, "Longing for God: Mother Teresa's Letters Reveal Isolation, Doubts," Catholicnews.com, March 1, 2002, http://www.catholic news.com/data/stories/cns/0201292.htm.

3. Jeff Wise, *Extreme Fear: The Science of Your Mind in Danger* (New York: Macmillan, 2009), 156–157.